The Formation Of Our Universe

Does Matter Really Matter?

James L. Shannon, PhD

To order additional copies of this book, contact:
Xlibris
844-714-8691
www.Xlibris.com
Orders@Xlibris.com

ISBN: Softcover   978-1-6641-9143-3
        EBook   978-1-6641-9144-0

Library of Congress Control Number: 2021917500

Print information available on the last page

Rev. date: 08/30/2021

Contents

ABOUT THE AUTHOR

BIRTHPLACE: Joplin, Missouri November 20,1937

MARRIED: January 1961 to Linda Kay Wickey (still am)

CHILKDREN:

Kenneth James: June 1962
Keith Brett: October 1963

EDUCATION

Bachelor of Science (Microbiology). California State University, Long Beach, California.

Master of Arts (Science Education-Emphasis Microbiology). California State University, Long Beach, California.

Doctor of Philosophy (Microbiology). Columbia Pacific University (non traditional)

RESEARCH AND PUBLICATIONS

1. Shannon, J.L., 1971. Transverse septum formation in budding cells of the yeast-like fungus *Candida albicans*. J. Bacteriol., 106:1026-1028.

2. Shannon, J.L. 1981. Scanning and transmission electron microscopy of *Candida albicans* chlamydospores. J. Gen Microbiol., 125:199-203.

3. Shannon, J.L., 1979. High school grades-how fair are plus and minus suffixes, J. Education, 100:153-157.

TEACHING CREDENTIALS:

California Secondary (Lifetime)
California Community College (Lifetime)
California Community College Administrative (Lifetime)

TEACHING EXPERIENCE

Advanced Placement Biology and Chemistry, University High School, Irvine, California
Anatomy and Physiology, Mount San Jacinto College, Menifee, California
Biology and Microbiology, California State University, Fullerton, California

THE TIMELINE

A hypothetical sequence of events)

Estimated "times". See "Chronology of the Universe" Wikipedia
What Existed Before the "Big Bang"?
No One knows.

A Big Bang Occurred
What Evidence Is There That A Big Bang Occurred?

Cosmic Wave Background?
An "Expanding" Universe?
Inorganic and Organic Composition of Our Universe?

How Was Our Universe Formed?

Was Matter Necessary?
Was our Universe Formed From "Nothing"?
Was only "energy" Required?

The Planet Earth Was Formed

No Doubt About This.
We all live on it.

Life on The Planet Earth

Was Life Formed From "Stardust"?
Was "Panspermia" responsible for Life On Earth?
Was "Creation" Responsible For life On Earth?

How Will Our Universe End??

No One Knows

WHAT DO YOU BELIEVE?

PREFACE

When I was fifteen years old, I looked at Saturn through a four-inch reflecting telescope. I was amazed at what I was viewing and asked an attendant how I could get a telescope of my own. I was told that I could build my own telescope from materials purchased from Cave Optical in Long Beach, California (no longer in business) and follow the instructions in Albert G. Ingall's book "Amateur Telescope Making" book one (which I did). I purchased a "mirror blank", set up "shop" in my parents garage and began grinding my own mirror.

One evening my father asked me what I was doing. I told him and he immediately became interested because of his profession as an optician. We became very close. Interestingly enough, there was an Individual that worked with my father who ground mirrors by hand and built telescopes. I had the best of all worlds when it came to advice and assistance.

My father died when he was 44 years old. II was a great loss for me to deal with, but it did not diminish my interest in astronomy and telescope building.

The years passed quickly and before I knew it two companies (Meade and Celestron) were formed. They manufactured professional grade telescopes for amateurs that are still manufactured today.

I later attended college and studied to be an astronomer but discovered that my skills in mathematics were simply not there. My interests then turned to biological sciences and years later I had earned a BS (Microbiology), an MA (Science Education) and a PhD (Microbiology). I began teaching high school advanced placement Biology and Chemistry, then community college, and then university Biology and Microbiology. All this never took away my interest in telescopes and astronomy.

Every time I used my telescope, I became more and more amazed at what I was looking at. How did all this matter get there? Was there a reason why this matter was arranged in such beautiful and recognizable constellations? Should I believe what theoretical physicists are telling me about the formation our universe and the "big bang"? What do they offer as undeniable proof? As a scientist myself, I began to question the "theories" theoretical physicists were telling us about the formation of our universe. They believe that our universe was formed about 13.8 billion years ago because of a "Big Bang" (a "singularity"), but how could they know this for sure? Does their **"evidence"** support their beliefs? Or were there flaws in their beliefs?

These unanswered questions increased my interest in how our universe was formed and were the inspiration for this book. Surely our universe was not formed because of random chance.

Theologians believe that God was responsible for the formation of our universe and base their beliefs on what the Bible says. **Scripture does support their beliefs**.

INTRODUCTION

What This Book Is All About

This book is not about science. It is about belief.

No one knows for sure how our universe was formed. Most theoretical physicists **believe** that it was formed because of the "laws" of physics about 13.8 billion years ago when a "region of extremely high temperature, density, and pressure exploded" (commonly referred to as the "Big Bang"). That is what **they** believe. In fact, theoretical physicists do not even sure that there was a specific "beginning" and that is why they work "backwards" from present day observations to when the big bang occurred.

What do **you** believe? Was our universe formed because of a "big bang" and the "laws" of physics, or was it formed by God as described in the Holy Bibles book of Genesis?

No one has an answer that is absolute proof for either of these questions.

The purpose of this book is to look at the "proof" theoretical physicists have (or do not have) about the formation of our universe.

Proof is defined as: "Evidence or argument establishing or helping to establish a fact or the **truth** of a statement".

So, how does one **prove** that the beginning of our universe was initiated by a "big bang"? The first thing that **must** be done is to **prove** where the extremely hot, dense matter for the big bang came from. **This has not been done.** Granted theoretical physicists have lots of observational data, such as the "Hubble Redshift", elemental composition of old and "newer" galaxies, and the cosmic wave background, **but none of these explain what the elemental composition of the big bang was, when it occurred,or <u>how this matter got there in the first place.</u> There is only conjecture. If theoretical physicists tell you that they do know, they are ignorant or not telling the truth.**

Some theoretical physicists even believe that our universe was formed from **nothing** ("ex nihilo" in Latin). An idea that is difficult, if not impossible, to prove.

You **do** have a choice about how our universe was formed. If you **believe** what theoretical physicists are telling us, ask them what reliable evidence do they have to support **their** beliefs? Guesses, ideas, conjecture, or unsupported theories are **not** admissible evidence!

Be careful about believing their "theories. Their theories are redundant and do not explain how their theories are obtained. The word hypothesis is virtually absent from their vocabulary.

If you have read the many books written by theoretical physicists about the formation of our universe, you have essentially read them all. They all contain the same information and, unfortunately, they are all very repetitious. Very few individuals outside the realm of theoretical physics are academically prepared to challenge the claims of theoretical physicists as they use only the "laws" of physics and mathematics to justify **their** beliefs. But is this enough to convince you and me who is **not** a theoretical physicist? Maybe. Maybe not

Do they expect everyone to already know what a theory is and how a theory is obtained? This book will explain what the scientific theory is; how a theory **MUST** be obtained.

Theoretical physicists are dogmatic about their theories and refuse to consider the possibility that our universe was created by God, or that religion and science may be compatible. This author believes science and religion **are** compatible. Einstein himself said that:

"Science without religion is lame", "Religion without Science is blind. All I want to know is how God thinks- the rest are mere details"[3].

Interesting insights from one of the most brilliant theoretical physicists of our time.

But what about God?

Dr. John Lennox tells us in his book *God's Undertaker. Has Science Buried God?"*[19] that "There is no more important debate than this-science versus religion. But it needs to begin again, with a clear understanding of what science and religion actually are". This book is lengthy and difficult to read. And, in this writer's opinion, there is too much history and little science to justify **his** beliefs. With respect to truth and **evidence** he quotes the following:

"It's not what you look at that matters, it's what you see" (something scientists call **evidence**).

"The next time that somebody tells you that something is true why not say to them what Richard Dawkins said: "What kind of **evidence is there for that? And if they cannot give you a good answer, I hope you'll think very carefully before you **believe** a word they say".

Bertrand Russell adds to this by saying:

"Whatever knowledge is attainable, it **must** be obtained by scientific methods; and what science cannot discover, mankind cannot know[27]"

So, the question must be asked; Is the big bang "theory" fact or fantasy? **It is not a fact. It is not even a theory. It is only a postulate** (Something suggested as true for the basis of reasoning, discussion, or belief.) **Wikipedia**

Perhaps everything we know in science is the result of God giving us answers to our questions as **He** sees fit. Indeed, if science had all the answers to our questions, and solutions to all of our problems, there would be no need for God. Scientists would eventually become omniscient.

Fortunately, omniscience is only held by God himself.

This book will:

1. Argue that **matter does matter**, and that it ***was* necessary at the site of the big bang in order for the formation of our universe.**

2. Argue that our universe could not have been formed from "nothing".

3. By simple example familiarize you with the scientific method and explain **how it is used every day of your life.**

4. Explain what a hypothesis is and why it **MUST come before a theory.**

5. Briefly discuss how life may have been formed on the planet Earth. Life got here, but how? Was it because of God, panspermia, directed panspermia, or even nothing?

6. Challenge you to think carefully and objectively about what you are being told by theoretical physicists, to use common logic (no mathematics!), **and to ask lots of questions.**

Do not be swayed one way or another with "theories" about the formation of our universe.

Is everything that theoretical physicists tell us factual? This author has the greatest respect for the contributions that theoretical physicists have made in an attempt to understand phenomena in our universe, and where we as humans fit into the "big picture".

You **DO** have a choice to believe or to not believe. What you **believe**, however, **must be based upon faith as well as knowledge.** But there is still so much we do not know. How much can we possibly know (epistemology)?

Every attempt has been made to keep this book as simple and readable as possible. Albert Einstein said that:

> "Everything should be made as simple as possible-
> but not simpler". This a major goal of this author.

So where do you go from here?

The first step on your journey is to **understand** "The Meaning of Belief" and why it is important.

CHAPTER ONE

THE MEANING AND IMPORTANCE OF BELIEF

What do **you** believe? Do you believe everything you are told, everything you see, or what you hear without asking any questions? Belief is a very personal thing. It is something that we all have engrained into our hearts and souls. No one has the same beliefs. They are something that is acquired when we are very young and as we get older. Belief is not something that we learn about in books or something you will find offered in college or university curricula.

Belief is defined as: **"The acceptance of truth of something. An acceptance by the mind that something is true or real, often underpinned by an emotional or spiritual sense of reality"** **(Wikipedia).**

Are you a skeptic?

A skeptic is "someone who has doubts about things that other people believe or habitually doubts, questions, or disagrees with assertions of generally accepted conclusions" **(Wikipedia)**

Dr. Steven Novella has written a book titled *"The Skeptics Guide to the Universe- How to Know What's Real in a World Increasingly Full of Fake"* [24]. This book is 446 pages long and very difficult to read without stopping and doing some independent research on the many topics he discusses. The only other alternative you have is to simply accept everything that Dr. Novella says is true.

Dr. Sean Carroll, theoretical physicist at the California Institute of Technology has reviewed Dr. Novella's book and states "There are so many ways to be wrong, and what we all need is a guidebook to being right. And here it is an invaluable manual to avoiding all of the ways we can fool ourselves and be fooled by others" (Inside cover of Dr. Novella's book).

Dr. Carroll is correct. There **are** many ways to be wrong, so **how can we be sure that something is right?** By proving that something is wrong- or "false"? Either way is a difficult, if not an impossible, task.

Dr. Neil DeGrasse Tyson, well known because of his involvement in television productions and a large number of published books has this to say about Dr. Novella's book: "Thorough, informative, and enlightening, the *"Skeptics Guide to the Universe"* inoculates you against the frailties and shortcomings of human cognition. If this book does not become required reading for us all, we **may** well see modern civilization unravel before our eyes"

Maybe. Maybe not.

Are you easily convinced, or are you a cynic?

A cynic is someone that denies all knowledge and is characterized by a general dstrust of others motives.

So, are you a skeptic or a cynic? Read Dr. Novella's book and decide for yourself.

James E. Alcock has written a book entitled *"Belief-What It Means To Believe and Why Our Convictions Are So Compelling"* [1] He tells us that "Our beliefs guide us, motivate us, and define the world for us", and asks the questions "How is it that some beliefs are so powerful that they are impervious both to reason and to evidence that challenges them?"

Theoretical physicists would like us to believe that there was elemental matter at the site of the "big bang", **but they have no actual proof of this**. At best, they only have guesses. Are guesses allowed by scientists? Yes, they are, but there is a difference between a "guess" and an "educated" guess.

A guess is: An opinion formed from **little or no evidence** ^{Wikipedia}

An educated guess is: An opinion that **requires supportive credible evidence.** It is called a **hypothesis** ^{Wikipedia}

Theologians would like us to *believe* in the Holy Bible: That "In the beginning God created the heavens and the Earth, and the Earth was without form and void" (Genesis 1:1)

Is there any actual "proof" of this? Does the Bible tell us anywhere that a "big bang" was responsible for the formation of our universe? No, it does not. There are, however, many places in the Bible that **are** supportive of a big bang (see the *"Life on Earth"* chapter in this book.

D.J. Kennedy has written a book titled *Why I Believe* that covers just about everything you can imagine[17].

It would appear that the words "belief" and "believe" should be key words in order to examine the formation of our universe, but the words "Belief/Believe" are not in the vocabulary of most theoretical physicists. They may use the word generically to say something like I believe I am getting weaker, but when it comes to theoretical physics their attitude changes drastically. As an example, the following question was recently asked on Quora (a question and answer forum on the Internet): "Do you completely believe in black holes, dark matter, and string theory?" It was answered on Quora on March 5, 2019 by physicist Viktor Toth who said:

"Believe"? "Completely"? "Sorry. I do not attend church".

Dr. Charles Stanley (Senior pastor of the television ministry *intouch.org*) tells us that belief begins in the mind and that **believe** is something that all of us do every day of our lives.

*We all **believe** that we will get to work safely, or we would never get in our car.

*We all **believe** that love will last forever, or we would never get married.

*We all **believe** that our favorite chair will support our weight, or we would never sit in it.

*Discussing what we **believe** with other others we trust is a way to better understand, collect fresh insights, and process information.

It is entirely probable that we will never know for sure how our universe was formed, either by the "laws" of physics, or as described in the Holy Bible until the return of Jesus Christ (When this happens, **and this author believes it will**, there will be a lot of theoretical physicists that will have red faces.)

Belief IS critical and is something that cannot be ignored. It is **NOT** a generic word that can be loosely bantered about.

CHAPTER 2

THE IMPROTANCE OF LANGUAGE

Definitions are important. Theoretical physicists use certain words in their language to describe what they *believe* happened before, during, and after the Big Bang, and to describe what is happening to our present day universe.

Words are just as powerful as mathematics. They are used to convey and clarify ideas, thoughts, methodology, and beliefs. Throughout this book several words are used to discuss the formation of our universe. Correct use of these words is critical if one is to describe the formation of our universe in an unbiased manner.

Refer to these definitions as you read this book.

Linguistics is the scientific study of language, and its form, meaning and context[Wikipedia]

Symantics is a part of Linguistics. It is the study of how words are used in language to convey ideas, thoughts, and beliefs [Wikipedia]

Meaning! Definition! Explanation!

Everything that you read can be interpreted differently, resulting in conclusions that are quite different. **The proper use of the English language is critical in order to correctly explain and interpret meaning and intent.**

According to Dr. Stephen Hawking, "Science questions become too technical and mathematical" and that Wittengenstein. the most famous philosopher of this century said "The remaining task for philosophy is the analysis of language[14]". This author agrees. That science becomes too technical and mathematical. Theoretical physicists need to take a course in linguistics and how words should be properly used, as the meaning of words and how they are used is critical in the credible justification of the "big bang".

Following are definitions of words that are important to understand their meaning and their proper use. They are, in some cases a direct quote from reliable sources, and in some cases a combination of direct quotes. They are here for your referral as needed.

Agnostic: Anyone who doesn't claim to know whether any gods exist or not.

Agnosticism: What a person does or does not know or believe.

Atheist: Someone who doesn't believe in ***any*** gods.

Arbitrary: Something that is based upon random choice or personal whim, rather than any reason or system.

Belief: Belief is the acceptance of truth of something. An acceptance by the mind that something is true or real, often underpinned by an emotional or spiritual sense of certainty.

Creation:

1. The act of making or producing something that **did not exist** before.

2. The act of making something that has **never been made** before.

Cynic: Someone whose attitude is characterized by a general distrust of others motives.

Evaluation: The highest level of the learning process. It is a systematic determination of a subject's merit, worth, and significance. It is used to determine the worth of any human endeavor. There are five steps in the learning process (lowest to highest): Comprehension, Application, Analysis, Synthesis; Evaluation.

Bloom's Taxonomy of Education

Evidence: An actual body of facts or information that indicates whether a belief or proposition is true or false.

Energy: There are many different forms of energy (mechanical, electrical, nuclear, chemical, etc.) but energy can be basically classified as either Kinetic (energy from movement) or potential (energy available to do work).

Epistomology: The ranch of philosophy of knowledge. The study of justification and the rationality of belief.

Entropy: A general trend of the universe towards death and disorder

Fact: Something that is indisputable. Something that cannot be denied.

Faith: The substance of things hoped for; the evidence of things not seen

(Hebrews 11:1 KJV Holy Bible).

Guess: An estimate or supposition about something **without sufficient information** of being sure of being correct.

Hypothesis:

1. A supposition or proposed explanation made on the basis of limited evidence as a starting point for further investigation.

2. A proposition made as a basis for reasoning, without any assumption of its truth.

Idea: An opinion, view, or belief.

Law: A statement based upon evidence obtained from repeated experimental observations. It describes some aspect of the world in which we live and it **always** applies under the same conditions and causal relationships involving its elements.

Model (Taken from Stephen Hawking's book *"The Grand Design"*[14]

A scientific model is a conceptual, mathematical or physical representation of a real world phenomenon. A model is generally constructed for an object or for a process when it is at least partially understood, but difficult to observe directly.

Nothing: Something that is nonexistent. The absence of anything and everything.

Opinion:

1. A view or judgment formed about something, *not* necessarily based upon fact or knowledge.

2. An estimation of the worth of something.

Origin: The point or place at which something comes into existence or the point or place where something comes from.

Phenomenon: A fact or situation that is observed to exist or happen, especially one whose cause or explanation is in question.

Philosophy: An academic discipline that exercises reason and logic in an attempt to understand reality and to answer fundamental questions about knowledge.

Postulate: A thing suggested as true for the basis for reasoning, discussion, or belief.

Proof:

1. A fact or **belief** that is accepted as true.

2. That which is true in accordance with fact or reality.

Probability:

1. The chance that a given event will occur.

2. A logical relation between statements such that evidence confirming one confirms the other to some degree.

Theory:

1. A supposition or a system of ideas intended to explain facts or events.

2. A careful examination of facts or phenomena.

3. A well established 8explanation for observations and scientific data.

Truth: A verified or indisputable fact.

CHAPTER 3

MATTER- WHAT IT IS AND WHY IT IS IMPORTANT

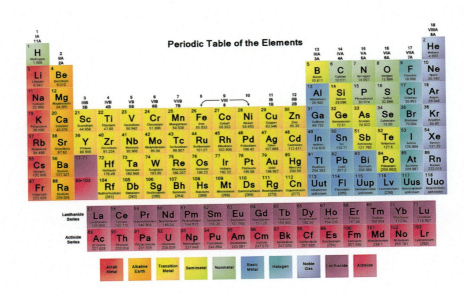

What is matter and where it came from is a very fundamental and important question.

Why? Because there **had to be matter present for a big bang to occur and for the formation of our universe.**

The presence of matter at the "site" of the big bang is something that theoretical physicists have not proved. They claim that they "know" what the composition of our universe was about one picosecond (10^{-12} seconds or .000000000001 seconds) **AFTER** the "big bang" occurred. But they have **absolutely no proof** about what kinds of matter were present when the big bang occurred.

The presence of matter is critical for the formation of our universe. There can be no guesses, assumptions, or speculations.

Matter is defined as **"Anything that occupies space and has mass". It is the "stuff" that makes up *everything* on the planet Earth. Its size or the way it behaves is not a consideration"** **Wikipedia**

There are five states of matter: Solids, Liquids, Gases, Plasma (an ionized gas), and the Bose-Einstein Condensate (a state of matter in which extremely cold atoms clump together and act as if they were a single atom).

The solid, liquid and gas states of matter are reversible and are easily demonstrated. These are the change of a solid into a liquid (ice into water), water changing into a gas (boiling water into steam), and steam changing back into liquid water (condensation). Plasma is easily recognized- we see it all around us, particularly with the use of ionized Neon in "Neon" signs. The Bose-Einstein condensate can only be demonstrated under controlled laboratory conditions.

Where is matter found? Matter is found everywhere. Above us, around us, beneath us, and inside of us. It makes up *everything* we see, touch, taste, breath and hear and collectively makes up everything on Earth-for both the living and non-living.

Historically, Dimitri Mendeleev arranged the first 63 known elements based upon their ascending atomic weight and similarities in chemical properties, which was published in *Principles of Chemistry* in 1869. The Periodic table today has 118 elements. The first 92 elements are naturally occurring, and the remainder are manmade. Mendeleev continued his work, became director of the bureau of weights and measurements in St. Petersburg, Russia until his death in 1907. The Periodic Table of the Elements is displayed on the walls of most school Chemistry and Physics classrooms, and the reasons *why* the periodic table is structured is carefully explained by teachers.

Dr. Neil DeGrasse Tyson and Dr. Donald Goldsmith's book *Origins* (Chapter 10 titled "The Elemental Zoo"[31]) discusses elements on the Periodic Table. This chapter is well written, informational, and easy to understand. In this book Drs. Tyson and Goldsmith **believe** that there was an "**abundant number of protons and electrons where the big bang occurred**". But how could they know this as fact? This is certainly speculation and an argumentative **belief**. They further state that hydrogen **gas** was made entirely during the first few minutes after the big bang occurred. Again, this is purely speculation, and not conclusive scientific evidence. They also **believe** there was an "abundant number of protons and electrons where the Big Bang occurred". This is an astounding statement. **How could this possibly be known?** What do they offer as proof? No-one actually observed a big bang, nor was anyone there to take a sample for laboratory analysis. So, where did the protons and electrons come from in order to make a hydrogen atom? (**Atomic** hydrogen is element number one on the periodic table. It consists of one positively charged proton in its nucleus (the Proton) and one negatively charged particle (the electron) which is found "outside" the nucleus. (**Molecular** hydrogen gas (H_2) is produced when two hydrogen atoms covalently bond by sharing their single electron

Hydrogen molecules can then undergo nuclear fusion to produce a Helium atom, and subsequent nuclear fusions can produce the heavier elements Lithium and Beryllium. Hydrogen and Helium are the two most prominent elements found in our universe.

Today, chemistry students are told about the characteristics of matter- their relative activity and how they form ionic and covalent bonds, but they are told nothing about the role matter must have played in the formation of our universe. Should they be told? What should they be told? Fact or we "believe"?

Will this book answer questions about the role elements may have played in the formation of our universe? No, but it will, *using only common sense and logic* (no mathematics or **"laws"** of physics) look at what theoretical physicists are telling us about where matter for a big bang had to come from. There is a difference of opinion. **Some** tell us that there was "**matter**" at the site of the big bang, **some** tell us there was "**nothing**" at the site of the big bang, and **some** tell us that there was only "**energy**" at the site of the big bang.

What a conundrum. Disagreement among theoretical physicists? This only leads us deeper into the unknown and results in even more questions that have not yet been answered. This is typical for science investigation. Disagreement among scientists is the fundamental fuel that causes them to continue their research.

In any event, do **you** believe that matter played an important role in the formation of our universe? **What it boils down to is what you believe, and what you believe should be based on undeniable fact, faith, and understandable, credible, and verifiable evidence obtained using the scientific method.**

Do you have an opinion? Do the answers given us by theoretical physicists satisfy your curiosity, or do we need more (and better) answers to our questions?

Yes, we do. We do need more and better answers.

According to Dr. Stephen Hawking (now deceased), probably the most recognized theoretical physicist in recent time, says that there was "nothing" where the big bang occurred and this "nothing" became "everything" in our universe over the course of approximately 13.8 billion years [15]

"Nothing" becoming "everything" is an interesting idea, but it leaves no room for anything else. This is a very narrow and opinionated **belief** that lacks any credible scientific proof. **How do you prove that "nothing" becomes "something" or even "everything"?** In the opinion of this author, matter **was** necessary for the formation of our universe. It had to be "there" when the big bang occurred. There can be no "ex nihilo" (something from nothing) formation- period. Simple logic tells me this is true.

What do you believe? Do you believe that you can get something from nothing?

Is matter necessary for the formation of our universe? If so, **WHERE DID IT COME FROM?**

CHAPTER FOUR

THE THEORY

Most people Have no idea what the scientific method is. Most believe that a scientific theory is simply a conjecture or a guess (something that is unsubstantiated and speculative), which is far from the truth.

Theories are used extensively by theoretical physicists to explain how our universe was formed. But what credible and verifiable scientific evidence do they have to support their theories?

Every scientific theory must start out as a hypothesis.

A hypothesis is sometimes referred to as an "educated" guess- a suggested solution for an unexplained observation that doesn't comply with a currently accepted theory. If enough evidence is collected to support a hypothesis, then the next step is to move to a theory. **If a multitude of tests always end up with the same conclusions, the theory may eventually become a scientific law.**

The University of California, Berkeley, defines a theory as "**A broad natural explanation for a wide range of phenomena. Theories are concise, coherent, systematic, predictive, and broadly applicable, often integrating and generalizing many <u>hypotheses</u>**"

So, it is extremely important to understand what a theory is. **It has a very important place in science.** Unfortunately, some theoretical physicists use "theories" ad infinitum without any verified evidence of how they were scientifically obtained. One must ask the question: **Is this theory justifiable on the basis of reliable and reproducible experimental evidence, such that it is not falsified, but proven truthful?**

A theory does not make factual claims- it must be a "**well substantiated explanation of some aspect of the natural world that is acquired _using the scientific method_ and is repeatedly confirmed through rigorous and comprehensive observation and experimentation**".

Repeatedly **confirmed?**

Not according to Dr. Karl Popper. Dr. popper wrote in his famous essay _"Science as Falsification"_, that every genuine test of a theory is an attempt to falsify, or refute it, and if any aspect of a theory or hypothesis can be falsified, then the hypothesis or theory is considered not true and must be modified[25].

Falsification is an absolute among theoretical physicists.

However, in this authors opinion, an equal amount of research **must be spent trying to prove a hypothesis true** as falsification of the hypothesis or theory will only be a chance event during the course of experimentation. This author never wasted valuable research time trying to prove that my doctoral hypothesis was false.

When it comes to the role of God in the formation of our universe, Richard Dawkins, an avowed atheist, says that **we should spend more of our time trying to prove that there is _no_ God**[9] (i.e., "**falsify**" God) which, of course he, or any other theoretical physicist or cosmologist cannot do- any more than they can "falsify" a theory about how our universe was actually formed.

Theories are used extensively by theoretical physicists to explain how our_universe was formed. But what credible and verifiable scientific evidence do they have to support their theories?

One thing is certain. A theory cannot be an "I believe", a "perhaps", a" maybe", a "suppose", or an "assumption" that has not been substantiated using the scientific method! These "theories" are not useful as they have not been sufficiently tested! Assumptions used to state a theory are probably the most incorrect part of a theory. They are used extensively. An assumption is "Something that is generally accepted without any evidence but cannot be proved as either true or false" [Wikipedia] Assumptions are especially dangerous as they have a tendency to lead the processing of thought in the wrong direction.

Is a "theory" valuable at all? Yes, a "good" theory establishes the foundation for the understanding of ***experimentally verified observational phenomena***. If a theory leads to a prediction and the prediction is experimentally verified, then the theory is strengthened. Theories must therefore be necessarily rigorous and comprehensive.

Can a theory be rejected or modified? Yes, **but only if those modifications are based upon new empirical and observational findings**. And, if experimental modifications are insufficient to support a theories prediction(s) then one must return to the scientific method to determine if the experimental design is sound. Fortunately, some theories are so well established that any new evidence from any source will not substantially change them. Examples of these are the cell theory and the atomic theory. Unfortunately, there are those that **believe** so much in **their** theory that they often **reinterpret it** so that what ***they*** believe in continually escapes being refuted. This kind of activity is not scientific and can keep a theory alive for some time.

The "bottom line" is this:

Theoretical physicists try to convince us that there is only one answer for the formation of our universe- the "Big Bang", and they will use the "laws" of physics and mathematics to "explain" virtually any question about the formation of our universe (Evidence for this is obvious when one reads answers to questions posted on "Quora", a web forum where theoretical physicists have "answered" any and all questions about our universe).

So, how do theoretical physicists define a theory?

Dr. Stephen Hawking says that a theory is a "good" theory if it satisfies two requirements: [15]

1. It must accurately describe a large class of observations on the basis of a model that contains only a few **arbitrary** elements.

   Definition of the word arbitrary is "**something *based upon random choice or personal whim***". Can "arbitrary" be allowed to describe an observation? In this authors opinion, It can **not**.

2. It must "make definite predictions about the results of **future** observations" (those that have not yet been observed, sic) and that "you can disprove a theory by finding even a single observation that disagrees with the predictions of the theory".

   Dr. Hawking's definition of a theory makes no mention of the importance of using the scientific method. This is probably an oversight on his part. I am certain he understood the importance of the steps necessary in the scientific method, and that they **cannot** be neglected. The scientific method **must** form the basis for every theory, but the first step in the scientific method–the statement of a "Hypothesis" seems to be a forgotten word in his (as well as others) vocabulary.

Dr. Hawking's concluding statement from his book *"A Brief History of Time"* [15] says:

"If we discover a complete theory it should in time be understandable in broad principle **by everyone**, not just a few scientists. Then we shall all, philosophers, scientists, and **just ordinary people**, be able to take part in a discussion of why it is that we and the universe exist. If we find the answer to that it would be the ultimate triumph of human reason-for **then we would truly know the mind of God**".

"Truly know the mind of God"? Was this an acknowledgement by Dr. Hawking that God does exist?

Albert Einstein one of the most brilliant theoretical physicists of our time said that "**I want to know God's thoughts- the rest are mere details**[3]".

Was this an acknowledgement By Einstein that God exists?

Albert Einstein defines the theory as something "that explains scientific observations" and that scientific theories must be falsifiable"[3] (Dr. Popper would be pleased).

Proving something "false" is not the end of scientific research. Hypotheses or theories can be improved or modified as more valid information is gathered, so that predictions will become more accurate over time.

A great deal of time **is** spent by todays theoretical physicists doing research, writing and publishing books, and hosting a variety of topics on television's Science channel in an attempt to convince everyone that ***their theories* are indeed *believable*.** While these programs are entertaining, they present little, **if any**, information how the scientific method was used to support their theories. This would take up too much airtime, and most viewers would probably be bored with this kind of information- Uuless they are well equipped with a thorough understanding of the scientific method.

The bottom line is this: A theory **must** be supported by reliable, reproducible and credible evidence collected from a variety of disciplines using the steps in the scientific method. If someone says to you "I have a theory", then demand that they present to you credible experimental evidence that has been obtained using the scientific method to support their "theory"!

An individual's academic excellence is not sufficient to result in a belief being presented and accepted as fact.

Ask a lot of questions and expect answers to these questions that are based upon sound, reliable, reproducible evidence.

In conclusion, we all have the right to believe what we wish to believe but be certain that what this belief **is based upon facts**- not theories. Be certain that you follow the following sequence of events for the formation of a theory. If this sequence breaks down at any point, then a theory cannot be used to make reasonable predictions.

1. **There must be multiple** similarities in credible observations that were obtained from a number of scientific disciplines (e.g., Astronomy, Physics, Mathematics; Chemistry)

2. From these credible observations **there must be a common problem recognition.**

3. From this common problem recognition one **must state a hypothesis** as a possible explanation for these observations.

4. Experiments must then be conducted (**with proper controls!**) that yields credible experimental evidence that that support the hypothesis.

5. This credible evidence can then be used to establish a "model"- **an idea that demonstrates common agreements** within these multiple scientific disciplines.

6. The model can then be used to state a "theory" which is a **possible explanation** for these common agreements.

7. The theory can then be used to make reasonable, testable predictions about future observations.

If anyone tells you "I have a theory", question them. Have them go through this check list. If they fail to have a _verifiable_ answer to any of these questions <u>in this sequence,</u> (you <u>cannot</u> jump around) then their "theory" needs a lot more work.

Bottom Line: Be aware of the multiple number of "theories" presented by theoretical physicists about the formation of our universe. Their theories **MUST** be supported by credible evidence that was collected using the scientific method!

ONLY THEN CAN YOU TRULY BELIEVE

CHAPTER FIVE

THE SCIENTIFIC METHOD

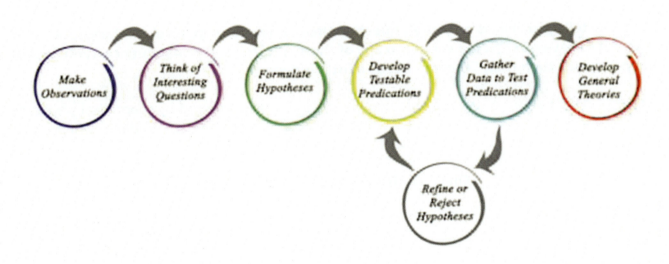

WHAT IT IS AND WHY IT IS IMPORTANT

While many readers of this book may be familiar with the scientific method, it is included here is a review. It is perhaps the most important chapter in this book. It will, by examples, illustrate how and why it **must** be used to arrive at a scientific theory.

The scientific method is a rigidly adhered to sequence of events that must be followed in

order to reach the level of the theory. <u>It eliminates ideas, guesses, opinions and suppositions as these will only lead to false conclusions and a dead end</u>.

In the scientific method a problem must first be identified by relevant **observations**. A **hypothesis** (an "educated guess") is then formulated from these observations which is **empirically tested using a *sequential* series of steps called experiments.** The results of these experiments are then carefully analyzed, and a decision is made whether or not the results support or "falsify" the hypothesis being tested.

Can the current "theory" about the formation of our universe stand up to the belief that our universe was formed by a big bang? In this author's opinion they cannot. A hypothesis for the formation of our universe has not been stated. Nor have any experiments been successful in an attempt to duplicate the big bang.

So, let's again make one thing very clear. **THE BIG BANG IS <u>NOT</u> A THEORY.** *It is only a postulate* (An idea or statement which someone believes or assumes to be true, although they may have no credible evidence for it).

Why is the Scientific Method Important?

The views of theoretical physicists about the formation of our universe are accepted by many people all over the planet earth. They have a great deal to say about what **they believe** to be true, **but is what they are telling us based upon reliable and reproducible, <u>evidence</u> that is consistent with observed phenomena obtained *using the scientific method*?** Make no mistake about this! Do not let anyone divert you from the correct use of the scientific method. In order to achieve relevant, consistent and reproducible results about the cause of an **observed** phenomena, and to establish whether the results are consistent with that observed phenomena *the scientific method must be followed.* If any "scientist" tries to tell you otherwise, they are not telling the truth. **There can be no deviation from this procedure!** One cannot simply say "I have a theory" because they have an observation, and have no substantial evidence obtained using the scientific method to falsify their theory.

The assumption is that the hypothesis about the formation of our universe is true until it is falsified.

German philosopher Dr. Karl Popper postulated that no amount of scientific data can really prove a theory, and that a single piece of key data could potentially disprove a theory (which is probably true). He wrote in his *Science as Falsification* essay that "The hallmark of a powerful **hypothesis**, perhaps the most critical component of the scientific method, is its vulnerability to falsification and not repeated verification", and that "hypotheses that are not "falsified" by experiments **may** be accepted as explanations for the observations made"[25]

Dr. Popper **believes** that in order for a hypothesis to be correct it must be falsified. If all efforts fail to falsify, **the hypothesis may then be considered to be correct, and when enough evidence has been collected to support the hypothesis it may then be considered a theory.** Bona fide theories are generally considered to be true, but they can still be proved incorrect as evidence collected in the future **may** alter its validity. A hypothesis, or a theory, cannot be both true and false at the same time- **the hypothesis must always come first.**

Dr. Popper also believes that falsification also applies to the validity of a **theory**. He claims that "**a theory or an idea shouldn't be described as scientific unless it could, in principle, be proven false**", which is what theoretical physicists adhere to. However, in this author's opinion, the same amount of effort should be put forth to prove a theory "true" as the amount of effort to prove it "false". **In this author's opinion, truth is just as powerful as falsification.**

Ashutosh Jogelakar has much more to say about falsification in his book *Falsification and its Discontents*[16], which is difficult reading.

Who are the best philosophers ever and why? The top nine are (percentage in order): Karl Marx 27.93 (first), David Hume, 12.67 (second), Ludwig Wittgenstein, 6.80 (Third), Friederich Nietzsche, 6.49 (fourth), Plato,5.65 (fifth), Immanuel Kant, 5.61 (sixth), Thomas Aquinas, 4.83 (seventh). Socrates. 4.82 (eight), Aristotle, 4.52 (ninth), and **Dr. Karl Popper, 4.20 (tenth). (Information posted on Quora by Paul Mainwood, Doctorate in Philosophy of Physics)**

You can view Dr. Popper's belief on the internet at *Karl Popper and Falsification.* (**https://www.youtube.com/watch?v=wf.sGgBsWv4**)

Can the current "theory" about the formation of our universe stand up to the belief that our universe was formed by a big bang? In this author's opinion they cannot. **A hypothesis for the formation of our universe has not been stated.** Nor have any experiments been successful in an attempt to duplicate the "big bang.

Why is the Scientific Method Important?

The views of theoretical physicists about the formation of our universe are accepted by many people all over the planet earth. They have a great deal to say about what **they believe** to be true, **but is what they are telling us based upon reliable and reproducible, <u>evidence </u>that is consistent with observed phenomena obtained *using the scientific method*?** Make no mistake about this! Do not let anyone divert you from the correct use of the scientific method. In order to achieve relevant, consistent and reproducible results about the cause of an **observed** phenomena, and to establish whether the results are consistent with that observed phenomena, **the scientific method must be followed.** If any "scientist" tries to tell you otherwise, they are not telling the truth. **There can be no deviation from this procedure!** One cannot simply say "I have a theory" because they have an observation, and have no substantial evidence obtained using the scientific method to falsify their theory.

Richard Dawkins in his book *The God Delusion*[9] is quoted as saying "The next time that somebody tells you that something is true why not say to them: What kind of evidence is there for that? And if they can't give you a good answer, I hope you'll think very carefully before you believe a word they say". Three words are critical in this statement and their definitions *are* important. *Truth* is a verified or indisputable *fact*. *Evidence* is the availability of facts or information indicating whether a belief or proposition *is* true or valid. A *Fact* is something that is consistent with reality or can be proved with evidence. **THE USUSAL TEST FOR A FACT IS VERIFIABILITY. NOT FALSIFICATION!**

Dr. Paul Davies (*The Mind of God-Science & the Search for Ultimate Meaning* [7] has also made the use, and importance, of the scientific method very clear by saying **"As a professional scientist I am fully committed to the scientific method of investigating the world"**.

Dr. John Lennox's book *"Gods Undertaker. Has Science Buried God?*[19] has correctly placed the "hypothesis" before the "theory". He has done an excellent job, but the book is lengthy and difficult to read, and there is too much emphasis on history and little science to justify many opinions.

There is a very original (and somewhat humorous) explanation in Dr. Lennox's book that explains the dilemma that exists among scientists and their beliefs about how our universe was formed. The example is called "Aunt Matilda's Cake". It is quoted here for your enlightenment.

"Aunt Matilda baked a 'beautiful cake'" and took it to be analyzed by a group of the world's top experts (a nutritionist, a biochemist, a chemist, a physicist, and a mathematician). They were asked to analyze the cake within the confines of their own academic disciplines and asked to give their report on "how" the cake was made and how its various constituent elements relate to each other. They did an excellent job explaining the structure of proteins and fats within the cake, the elements involved and their chemical bonding, the fundamental particles that are present and the mathematicians who offered a set of elegant equations to describe the behavior of the elegant particles. But when they were asked "Why was the cake made?" They did not have an answer. The grin on Aunt Matilda's face indicated that only she knew the answer-she made it for a purpose." The scientists could not have known the answer to this question. All anyone had to do was ask Aunt Matilda for the answer to the "why" question. This conclusion from this example that science is "the only way to truth" is **patently false**, is an excellent illustration of "how" science functions, and why science does not have all the answers to our "why" questions.

So, should you believe the theories that science asks us to believe? Are all the explanations that science gives us the truth? What **YOU believe** is entirely up to you.

Bertrand Russell supports Dr. Lennox by saying that "While it is true that science cannot decide questions of value, that is they cannot be intellectually decided at all, and lie outside the realm of truth and falsehood. Whatever knowledge is attainable, **must be obtained by scientific methods; and what science cannot discover, mankind cannot know and what science cannot discover, mankind cannot know**"[27]

Physics, Chemistry, and Biology students are taught early in their studies that the scientific method is a fundamental and imperative part of problem solving and why it **must** be used in order to find a solution to an observed problem in a rational, explainable, understandable, reproducible, and verifiable method using laboratory tests called experiments which is, in this author's opinion, the most critical component of the scientific method.

Perhaps it has been some time since you have taken a Chemistry, Biology or Physics class. Perhaps you have never been involved in scientific research. If that is the case, a brief review of the sequence of events that *must* be used in the scientific method is relevant in order to understand and challenge the theories of theoretical physicists. These steps **cannot** be questioned or modified, and **there is no room for deviation**.

The best way to explain the scientific method is by example (which, in this author's opinion is always the preferred method of teaching). The following is a very simplistic example. It has nothing to do with science, per se, but it does illustrate how the scientific method is used every day of our lives.

Step 1. Observation/Problem Recognition

Your automobile engine will not start (something we all have probably experienced sometime in our life). **This is a problem, and it was recognized when you tried to start the engine!**

Step 2. The Hypothesis

A hypothesis is often referred to as an "**educated guess**". A guess that offers a **_possible_** solution to a problem.

Albert Einstein himself said the following about the hypothesis:

"For me, a hypothesis is a statement whose truth is **temporarily** assumed, but whose meaning must be beyond all doubt"[3].

In this example, a reasonable hypothesis why the automobile engine will not start might be is: **The automobile battery is dead.**

Step 3. The Experiment

An experiment is a carefully planned test that is used to obtain credible and reproducible evidence that may, or may not, support a hypothesis. They are always done under "controlled" conditions. In other words, you must always be aware of what variables **may** contribute to the problem, and these variables must always be controlled so that you are certain the results you are seeing is truly because of what you have proposed in the hypothesis.

Example: The battery is dead and needs to be charged (or replaced with a new battery). So, you have the battery charged (an experiment) and try to start the engine. The engine still will not start. The Hypothesis is therefore not supported.

A new hypothesis may, or may not, be necessary as there may be something wrong with the experimental design.

However, before throwing out your hypothesis, the next step would be to revise your experiment- A good revision here would be to replace the dead battery with a new battery to see if the engine will now start.

Step 4. Experimental Result(s)

You installed a new battery and the engine started! Congratulations! In this example, replacement of the dead battery with a new battery started the automobile engine. This evidence supports the hypothesis.

Step 5. Conclusion(s)

Conclusions are essentially the outcome of an experiment and are drawn from the examination of experimental results. These conclusions may be placed into one of three categories:

a. The conclusions always support the hypothesis. The hypothesis is undeniably true and is where every scientist would like the results of experimentation to end. The conclusion is indisputable! **No** experiment can be conducted to disprove the hypothesis!

b. The conclusions do not support the hypothesis. The hypothesis is not true.

This is where every scientist does not want to end! Who wants to spend years of research trying to prove something that can not be proved? Or, for that matter, trying to falsify (disprove) something as Dr. Karl Popper would like us to believe.

c. The conclusions may seem to have some components that support the hypothesis, but more testing (experiments) must be done.

In this example the battery ("a") is the obvious problem and there is no need for further experimentation.

It should be noted that a flaw in experimental design can easily account for outcome "c", and simple change(s) in an experimental design may ultimately lead to an "a" outcome. If you do not believe this, ask any doctoral degree candidate how many times they have changed an experimental design before getting results that are so supportive of their hypothesis and so convincing that to argue against it is futile. **Aren't they in essence trying to prove their hypothesis is true rather than prove it false**? Total and complete falsification" at every step of their investigation means the candidate will probably ever prove their thesis and never obtain their advanced degree!

When a hypothesis is tested in many different ways (**in multiple disciplines as necessary**) and they all end up with the same conclusion, **the hypothesis may then be used to develop a "model".**

The definition of a scientific "model" is "**the generation of a physical, conceptual, or mathematical representation of a real phenomenon that is _difficult to observe directly._ They are at best approximations of the objects and systems that they represent-they are _not_ exact replicas**" Wikipedia

This model can then justifiably be tested in a number of different ways to produce a theory (or theories) which may then be used make predictions.

So, there you have it. There is nothing mysterious about understanding and applying the scientific method to problem solving.

Theoretical physicists seem to come up with lots of models, theories, and predictions that are **not** based upon the use of the scientific method. They go directly from an observation to a "theory", **bypassing** the steps in the scientific method necessary to reach the point where the statement of their theory and models they come up with are supportive of their beliefs and assumptions. This is not justifiable or even allowable!

Example of a failing battery is a very simplistic example, but it does illustrate the necessity of following the steps in the scientific method and not jumping directly to a conclusion without supportive experimental evidence. Yet, in all the books this author has read, **none of the steps in the scientific method are outlined**, explained. or discussed. Theoretical physicists come up with models, theories, and predictions that are *not* supported by the use of the scientific method. Jumping to a theory **before** the hypothesis seems to be quite common! As a matter of fact, in all the books that this author has read the word hypothesis is rarely mentioned! It is always" I have (or we have) a "theory" right away. This is, in this author's opinion, not acceptable science.

The best example of the scientific method is the work done By. Dr. Edwin Hubble[12] in 1929 Dr. Hubble used the 100-inch Hooker telescope on top of Mt. Wilson in Southern California to show that galaxies were moving away from each other. Dr. Hubble used a spectral technique called the "redshift" that demonstrated that our galaxies were apparently moving away from each other (an "expansion"). This rate of galaxy expansion was expected to slow down because of entropy (a loss of energy to support an infinite expansion as objects increased their distance between each other). As energy was lost in the expansion, it was thought that galaxies would begin to slow down and ultimately return to their original point where the big bang occurred (a process that has been called the "big crunch"). But this is not the case. Galaxies are not slowing down- **they are speeding up!**

Dr. Hubble used the scientific method exactly as it should be used! He proved that it works and that it cannot be modified to satisfy the whim and fancy of anyone simply to make "science" work on their behalf! **He certainly did not try to prove his observations false.** Of course, Dr. Karl Popper would disagree with Dr. Hubble's methodology.!

This author is astonished how theoretical physicists try to justify **their** beliefs by saying "I have a theory" **with absolutely no presentation of a hypothesis, or any experimental evidence that allows them to arrive at a correct conclusion that allows them to "prove" OR "falsify".** It is unacceptable to say, "I have a theory" without first stating a hypothesis, and the obtaining substantial experimental evidence to advance their hypothesis to a "theory"! If you find this difficult to believe, examine the books written about the formation of our universe (a tedious and time-consuming task), and watch (and **LISTEN**) to the entertaining science presentations on television. Count the number of times "I have a hypothesis" is said (there are virtually none) versus how many times "I have a theory" is said (there are many).

What evidence do theoretical physicists have to validate a "Big Bang"? There are three, but the major argument for the formation of our universe is the "discovery" of the osmic wave background (CWB).

1. The Cosmic Wave Background (CWB)

The cosmic wave background (CWB) is a "relic" created supposedly from the big bang explosion. Penzias and Wilson won the Nobel prize in physics in 1969 for the identification and verification of the CWB [Wikipedia]. Is this enough substantial information to say with any certainty that the CWB was *in fact* produced by a big bang? Maybe. Maybe not. Or is it a supposition? (**A supposition is "An idea or theory you *believe* to be true even though you do not have enough proof"**)

How was the CWB produced? The story goes something like this.

There was once upon a time a region in space that was extremely dense with a large concentration of protons, electrons, positrons, neutrinos, and perhaps other subatomic particles. This is supposedly the region (or regions if you believe that the big bang was an explosion that occurred "everywhere"), and that this explosion was a "**point**" of infinite density composed of high energy subatomic particles. Is there any proof of the existence of subatomic particles at the region of the big bang? No, there is not. **Is there any reliable experimentation that proves that the CWB actually originated from a "point" or "everywhere" where a big bang may have occurred? No, there is not.**

As a matter of fact, proof of the Cosmic Wave Background has been challenged by University of Alabama theoretical physicists in a paper titled "**Big Bang's Afterglow Fails Intergalactic 'Shadow' Test'**" *Science Daily, 5 September 2006*. The published summary states: "The apparent absence of shadows where shadows were expected to be is raising new questions about the faint glow of microwave radiation once hailed as proof that the universe was created by a "big bang". In a finding sure to cause controversy, scientists at the University of Alabama in Huntsville (UAH) found a lack of evidence of shadows from "nearby clusters" of galaxies using new, highly accurate measurements of the cosmic wave background".

So, who should you believe? Why should you believe?

2. An Expanding Universe

Our universe **is** expanding. No one challenges Dr. Hubble's work (see Hubble's Red Shift experiment).

3. The presence of water, dust, and other types of matter spread throughout our universe.

All of these have been experimentally proved to exist in our universe, **but how they got there has NOT been proved.**

Some researchers, unfortunately, make unreliable false assumptions about their observations and then spend many years trying to prove something that simply can not be proved. These assumptions are often not discarded because of lack of reliable information- they are simply modified to meet the "needs" of the investigator which keeps the wheels in motion. This is **NOT** good science.

One thing that is done masterfully by theoretical physicists is to spread their theories world-wide on television and computer programs. They have only one goal- to convince you that our universe was created by a big bang. The images they show are very impressive. But can a computer simulate what **may** have happened at the site of a big bang? Yes, they can do this. But are these images real or simply imagination?

In conclusion, the scientific method is something that is indisputable and can not be dismissed in establishing the validity of a big bang. **Every single step MUST be verified time and time again using a variety of methods and they MUST arrive at the same conclusion**. Nor can the scientific method be tampered with in any way in an attempt to justify the theoretical physicists' "belief" that a big bang actually did occur.

It is your privilege to believe that "falsification" is the way to establish truth. In this author's opinion the only way to truth is verification not falsification.

Whether or not our universe was formed by a big bang or if it was created by God is simply a belief. Perhaps there is a God that has everything all planned and thought out and He is simply providing theoretical physicists (and cosmologists) with bits and pieces about the formation of our universe. – when and how as He sees fit.

God and science, in this authors opinion, are compatible.

CHAPTER SIX

THE FORMATION OF OUR UNIVERSE

In The Beginning

The "Laws of Physics" created the Universe

In The Beginning There Was "Nothing"

God Created The Heavens and The Earth- Genesis 1:1

The term "Big Bang" was introduced by the astronomer Fred Hoyle in a 1949 BBC radio broadcast. This name has remained with us since that time. Supposedly the big bang was not an explosion that spreads material outwards like the exploding stick of dynamite. Rather, it was an initial "singularity"- a "time"- which is difficult to explain and understand. Regardless of this the "big bang" **is** referred to as an explosion in the many repetitious books written by theoretical physicists. They may have differences in finite areas, but the information they provide is essentially the same. They seem to have made the big bang a form of scientific "religion".

The Encyclopedia Britannica states the big bang is a: "Widely held theory of the evolution of the universe. Its essential feature is the emergence of the universe from a state of extremely high temperature and density- the so-called big bang that occurred at least 10,000,000 years ago" Theoretical physicists now tell us it was closer to 13.8 billion years ago.

It should be noted that even Einstein doubted the Big Bang [Quora].

If the Big Bang made the universe, then what exploded? Good question.

Kristen Sundelin UX writer at HiQ Goteborg (2011-present) answered this question on Quora as follows:

"The Big Bang wasn't an explosion. It was a rapid expansion of space. And the Big Bang theory doesn't describe how something comes from nothing, but how we got from a very hot very dense state to the very empty an cold space.

A rapid expansion of space? How would you define "space"?

How something comes from nothing cannot be described? Of course it can't. How would you define "nothing"?

How we got from a very hot, very dense state to the present state is still unknown.

Sundelin goes on to say "Exactly how it happened is still unknown, but there is a lot of evidence that it did. We see the expansion as it happens today in the form of redshift, and we see traces of the early expansion in the ripples in the cosmic wave background radiation".

A lot of evidence? Granted an expansion is good scientific evidence (Edwin Hubble and the red shift), but the cosmic wave background has been challenged simply because there is no proof that there was any matter for the formation of our universe in the first place.

Sundelin continues "We can **infer** and simulate what happened before (the big bang, sic) thanks to physics and tests in particle colliders. But even that has its limits:

The Planck Epoch, the first 10^{-43} seconds of the universe, where conditions are so extreme that the fundamental forces of gravity has to combine with the other three (electromagnetic force, weak nuclear force and strong nuclear force). The problem is that gravity is governed by general relativity, and the other three by quantum mechanics- and those two do not play nice. We need a new physics theory to combine them- a theory of everything........**and we don't have one**"

'So in the end, because of these physical barriers, we can see that he expansion od space happened, but we cannot figure out why- yet".

Of course, is it possible that the big bang could be false? If so, what other theories could also be feasible? Viktor T. Toth, IT pro, part-time physicist answered this question on Quora as follows:

"Of course it is possible that a physical theory is false"

"Science is not religion. Though we seek truth (an understanding of Nature) we do not claim to know the absolute truth. Sure, some theories are better tested than others, but ultimately, given that we only can ever make a finite number of observations, exceptions are always possible, unaccounted for by existing theory".

"So while it is unlikely that the big bang model (that is to say an expanding universe with a hot and dense past) is grossly wrong, our understanding has a long way to go when it comes to its detailed features".

A long way to go to understand its detailed features? This is a polite way to say we don't understand everything and it will be a long time before we do.

This author agrees.

But what about what we are told in the Holy Bible?

The Holy Bible tells us that our universe was **created** by the hand of God.

But whom do you **believe**? Theoretical physicists or the Bible? And **why** do you believe what you believe what you believe? No one denies that our universe was formed. We all live in it, but **how** it was formed, **where** it was formed, and **where the matter came from to form it** are questions that remain unanswered.

Was our universe formed or was it created?

The definition of belief is **"The state of believing; a conviction or acceptance that certain things are for real; a condition in which an individual holds a conjecture or premise to be true"** Wikipedia

The definition of creation is: **"The act of making or producing something that did not exist before"; "the act of making something that has never been made before"** Wikipedia

Use of the word "belief" or "believe" to explain how our universe was formed is not in the vocabulary of most theoretical physicists. If or when it is used is often used incorrectly.Viktor Toth, IT, and part-time physicist who regularly answers theoretical physics questions on *Quora*, an internet question and answer forum, says "Believe? "When it comes to science, I do not use the language of roadside preachers" and that "everything in our universe can be explained using the laws of physics and mathematics". But is this a scientific fact or fantasy?

What about belief? Does belief require tangible evidence? Not necessarily. For example, this author can **believe** that the planet Earth will be destroyed by a comet impact in the next 100 years or that the state of California will be split in half sometime in the future by a horrendous earthquake. There is no basis in fact for these beliefs, but it is my privilege to believe whatever I wish to believe.

What about scientific fact? A fact is something that is indisputable. It is the outcome of verifiable experimental evidence obtained from a testable hypothesis which produces irrefutable conclusions. For example, Kepler's Laws are fact, but to say that mathematics can explain *every* observable phenomenon in our universe is a huge assumption...

What "facts" do theoretical physicists have about the big bang? Very few, if any. Here are some of reasons why:

1. They do not know for certain what types of matter were actually present at the site of the Big Bang. **If they say that they do know, they are not telling the truth.**

2. They cannot experimentally prove that there was "nothing", "something", or only "energy" at the site of the Big Bang.

3. They cannot duplicate what the big bang may have been like in the laboratory because **they do not know what it was actually like.**

4. They have no actual measurements of temperature and pressure at the site of the Big Bang, **nor have they experimentally produced these conditions in the laboratory.**

5. They have no actual images of the Big Bang. The images they show in books and on television programs are only **what they think the Big Bang may have looked like.**

6. **They cannot identify precisely where the Big Bang occurred**- if it was a "**point** of extremely high density and pressure" or if it occurred "**everywhere**" as they claim.

7. They rely only upon mathematics to justify their "theories" and "conclusions".

8. They construct "models" based upon "observations" and then use these models to produce "theories" **which may or may not be valid.**

9. "**Predictions**" are then made based upon their theories.

10. If their predictions are not supported by conclusive experimental evidence, **they can simply modify their model until it does support their theory**. (It should be noted that a "model" can be easily modified, and if modification is done enough times, there is a good chance that someday that modification will meet their needs which is an inappropriate approach to problem solving.)

11. **The very core belief in the Big Bang has been questioned by a leading group of concerned scientists**. Their concerns were outlined in "*An Open Letter to The Scientific Community*"[29] The journal *Nature* rejected this letter for open publication.

Why was this paper rejected? Your guess is as good as mine, but the list of competent scientists that reject the big bang "theory" is very impressive.

Regardless of these reasons, theoretical physicists tell us that they know what the composition of our universe was- right down to the last picosecond (0.000000000001 second, or 10^{-12} second) **after** a Big Bang occurred. How can they be certain of this with such precision? They also say that our universe could have popped into existence 13.8 billion years ago without any divine help. They say we should simply trust the laws of physics.

Carl Wieland has written a paper in which secular scientists blast the big bang[33]

Sarfarti[28] has written an excellent book that addresses the importance of making assumptions about the big bang and astronomy.

Dr. Steven Weinberg, winner of the 1979 Nobel Prize in Physics in his book *"The First Three Minutes"*[32] writes the following about matter and the Big Bang [s]

"There was an explosion in which a single hot and very dense **point** in space explodes and begins to expand outward, creating space and time. This **explosion** occurred simultaneously **everywhere**, filling all space from the beginning, with every particle of matter rushing apart from every other particle. But this **explosion** was not like an explosion like those familiar on Earth, starting from a definite center and spreading out to engulf more and more of the circumambient air, **but an explosion which occurred everywhere** filling all space from the beginning with every part of matter rushing apart from every other particle" and "the matter rushing apart in this explosion consisted of various types of elementary particles which are the study of modern high-energy nuclear physics. One type of particle that was present in large numbers is the electron-the negatively charges particle that makes up the outer parts of all atoms in the present universe".

Dr. Weinberg's language seems to be somewhat contradictory. He states that there was "a **single** hot and very dense **point** in space" but then states that the big bang explosion happened **everywhere**? Which was it? A single point or was it everywhere? A point cannot be everywhere! (Although theoretical physicists will probably challenge this).

A point is defined as: **"A single localized source of something"**.

Dr. Weinberg continues to explain that in the first three minutes our universe "is **filled with an undifferentiated soup of matter and radiation**". The existence of **matter** at the site of the big bang is patently admitted by Dr. Weinberg. But how could he know this? He could not. **It is, at best, only a guess.** In fact Dr. Weinberg adds the following caveat to what he has written by saying **"I cannot deny a feeling of unreality on writing about the first three minutes as if we really know what we are talking about"** and further admits that **"I am not sure about the first three minutes, but this is as good a guess as any"**.

How good a guess this is remains to be proved.

Do other theoretical physicists feel the same as Dr. Weinberg? Yes. Dr. Stephen Hawking has this to say in his book *The Theory of Everything*"[13] "The history of our universe is known as the hot big bang model" and that our universe is described by a "Friedman model right back to the big bang. In the Friedman "model" **the universe expands**. The temperature of **matter** in it will go down and this cooling "will have a major effect on **this matter** ". "The initial rate of expansion must have been very carefully chosen" and that "it would be very difficult to explain why the universe should have begun in just this way, except as an act of a **g**od who intended to create beings like us". (Note that Dr. Hawking said the act of a **g**od (lower case "g") who intended to create beings like us, not the act of **G**od (Upper case "G") which is indicative of his belief about the role God may have had in the formation of our universe). Again, "**matter**" is patently admitted.

Dr. Hawking goes on to explain that "As the universe expanded the matter particles got further apart and that about one second after the big bang its temperature would have fallen to about ten thousand million degrees- about a thousand times the temperature of our sun's center". He further states that "The universe at this time would have consisted mostly of photons, neutrinos and their antiparticles, with some protons and neutrons. The protons and neutrons would begin to collide when the temperature falls to about one thousand million degrees at which time, they would begin to combine with each other to produce the nuclei of "**heavy**" hydrogen. These "heavy" hydrogen molecules would then begin to combine with more protons and neutrons to produce small amounts of Lithium and Beryllium", and that "inflation could also explain why there is so much **matter** in the universe which further justifies that the total energy of the universe is zero and that classical theory is no longer a good description of the universe, so one has to use a **quantum theory of gravity** to discuss the very early stage of the universe".

Just where did the photons, neutrinos, protons, and neutrons come from? Did they just appear out of a clear blue sky? Do you believe that you can get something from nothing? (See the chapter in this book titled "Something from Nothing?" – a book by this title has been written by Dr. Leonard Krauss[18])

The average person on the street has no idea what Dr. Hawking is talking about, and no attempt will be made here to paraphrase what he has said. **The quantum theory of gravity is yet to be proved.**

Dr. Hawking summarizes his "beliefs" as follows:

1. "God may know how the universe **began** (note he did not say how **God** created the universe, as this implies that God was involved in its beginning), but we can not give any particular reason for thinking it began one way or another. In fact, the boundary condition of the universe is that it has no boundary. The universe would be completely self-contained and not affected by anything outside itself. It would neither be created nor destroyed. **It would just be**".

   It would just be? How could Dr. Hawking, or anyone else, have any evidence that our universe has "no boundary". It appears to this author that Dr. Hawking, as well as many other theoretical physicists, would have to be somewhat omniscient to make such a claim.

2. "The singularity theorems of classical general relativity showed that the universe **must** have a beginning and that the beginning must be described in terms of quantum theory".

   ***Must* be described in terms of quantum theory?** The use of the word **must imply that there is no alternative to the beginning of our universe-period.**

3. **If** the universe is really self contained having no boundary or edge, it would be neither created nor destroyed".

   Again, is this an idea, a guess, a belief, an assumption, or a speculation? **The use of the word "If" indicates pure speculation** and releases Dr. Hawking from providing any degree of certainty or proof.

4. "It would simply be. What place then for a creator?" How can Dr. Hawking even address the **place** of a creator when he refuses to consider that a creator even exists, let alone address His "place" in the universe?

    Obviously, Dr. Hawking does not believe in God. But could Dr. Hawking have given us more in his lifetime had he incorporated (or even considered) God's possible role in the formation of our universe? We will never know. One thing is certain, he, as well as almost all theoretical physicists, believe that all of the theoretical questions about "everything" in our universe can be explained using the "laws" of physics and that

Someday a "unified field theory" will explain "everything". It is interesting to note that Albert Einstein was working on this "unified field theory" until his death in 1955- with no success.

To be fair, there are some theoretical physicists that believe a creator did have a role in the formation of our universe. A survey conducted by the PEW Research Center (June 2009) tells us that chemists are more likely to believe in God (41%); scientists are roughly half as likely as the general public to believe in God or a higher power than those who are older".

One of these theoretical physicists has stated "Is the unified field theory so compelling that it brings about its own existence? Or does it need a creator and, if so, does He have any effect on the universe other than being responsible for its existence? And who created Him?"

And who created Him? An excellent question. If it could be answered, the next question by theoretical physicists would logically be: "Who created the "Him" that created the present "Him". This repetitious question will never reveal who "Him" is. The question is exactly the same as the question "Which came first the chicken or the egg?" There is no answer.

According to Dr. Hawking "science questions become too technical and mathematical" and that "Wittgenstein, the most famous philosopher of this century" (which is debatable). Wittgenstein of our time ranks tenth in a poll of the most "famous" philosophers and said that the remaining task for philosophy is **the analysis of language**". This author completely agrees. Theoretical physicists need to take a good course in linguistics (the study of language) and examine how words should be properly used (semantics). The meaning of words and how they are used is critical to explain any scientific phenomena –not just the big bang.

Can our universe continue to expand ad infinitum? Will there be another "big bang"? Who knows? Some theoretical physicists have postulated that there will come a time where gravitational attraction between objects in space would diminish to a point that these expanding objects will reverse their direction and move backwards towards their place of origin, resulting in a "big crunch" which is only a guess. In fact, our universe **is** expanding!

If the Big Bang was created from an infinitely small space, in what space did that infinitely small spot reside? Where is that place today? No one knows. No one even knows where a "point" or "everywhere" was when the big bang occurred.

Victor Toth, IT and part-time physicist who regularly posts answers to theoretical physics questions on Qoura says: "No, the Big Bang was not created from an infinitely small spot. Not true. **Something may have been created**, but the amount of **matter** must not change". The first thing that must be done is to **eliminate all of the higher mathematics and simply rely upon logic**". He further states that physicists believe that the formation of our universe can be explained using "mathematics" and that they keep on trying to come up with a "unified field theory" that will mathematically explain "everything", and they continue to pursue this because this is "what the equations tell us".

Amazing. A theoretical physicist telling us that something may have been **created**, and that we **must eliminate all of the higher mathematics and simply rely upon logic**?

Toth candidly admits that if theoretical physicists were to truthfully answer the question where did **matter** come from, they would have to answer, "**We are not certain about anything**", He continues to tell us that "As to where the big bang happened.......... everywhere. **It is not a location in space. It is a moment in time**. And this is not some figure of speech. This is precisely what the equations tell us, too. Which describes a universe that is infinite in space" and "very simply the equations describe a universe that is infinite in space approximately the same everywhere (homogeneous) and has no preferred direction (isotropic). These properties do not change over time. **The only thing that changes over time is the matter density in this infinite universe**. Early on it was very high; **it has been decreasing ever since**. Everywhere".

"Time" is mentioned three times. Supposedly "time" (t=0) **began** when the "singularity occurred. When time "began" is up for grabs. How would you define "time"?

It is interesting to note that "young" PhD theoretical physics students today learn to keep silent if they have something negative to say about the big bang standard model. To challenge the ruling big bang paradigm and the beliefs of the academic elite could be fatal to their future.

Will we ever be able to discover what was **before** the big bang? Maybe, but don't hold your breath.

There is so much that we do not know, Will we ever know? Will there ever be a need to know?

Maybe. Maybe not. Hopefully this book will allow the casual reader to understand (and perhaps challenge) what theoretical physicists have told us about the formation of our universe and to better understand what they will tell us in the future.

Belief is a critical component of understanding.

CHAPTER SEVEN

SOMETHING FROM NOTHING?

Some theoretical physicists believe that" nothing" is required for the formation of our universe. This requires lots of speculation and magination. To prove that "nothing" exists or that "nothing" can become "something" would be difficult, if not impossible to do. Proof is the key ingredient.

If there was absolutely nothing billions of years ago, wouldn't there still be absolutely nothing now?"

Can you find anything in published literature that **proves** that nothing can become something? None that that author is aware of.

Dr. Lawrence Krauss, an internationally known theoretical physicist has written a lengthy book entitled *"A Universe from Nothing"* [18]. It goes to great length (191 pages to be exact) to convince you and I that our universe was "**created**" from "**nothing**". He further claims that he has "provocative" answers to the questions "Where did the universe come from"? "What will the future bring?" and "Why is there something rather than nothing"? He identifies these questions as the "need for first cause", and that the declaration of a first cause leaves opens the question "Who created the creator" and who created the creator that created the creator. He states that surely **nothing"** **is every bit as physical as "something,** especially if nothing is defined as "the absence of something", and suggests that "not only can something arise from nothing, something will *always* arise from nothing" and argues that "if there is the potential to create something then that is not a true state of nothingness, and that there is a "deeper kind of nothing, which consists of no space at all, and no time, no particles, no fields, no laws of nature", and "That to me is as close to nothing as you can get". Honestly, this author does not at all understand a word of this.

Dr. Krauss' book is also quite clear as to his conviction about the creation of our universe by a creator. He says" I must admit that I am *not* sympathetic to the conviction that creation requires a creator, which is at the basis of all of the world's religions". and continues to say that "many laypeople as well as scientists revel in our ability to explain how snowflakes and rainbows spontaneously appear, based upon **simple, elegant laws of physics".** He further states that the reason his book was written was "to give the answers that are suggested by recent discoveries and theoretical advances" and to inform us that "**we have a great many universes created out of nothing".**

A great many universes created out of nothing? Identify just one of them.

Dr. Neil DeGrasse Tyson agrees when he says that "Nothing is not nothing. Nothing is something. That's how a cosmos can be spawned from the void"[31] He has written a review of Dr. Krauss' book which includes many other opinions from individuals in many other academic disciplines. Many reviewers have classified this discussion as a "kerfuffle" (a lot of argument, noisy activity, or fuss). He continues to say that "It's a shame when smart people who agree about most important things can't disagree about some other things without throwing around insults. We should strive to do be better than that". He further admits on *Science Friday* that "cosmologists.... sometimes exaggerate a little bit about what it (the Big Bang, sic) means.

He may be right.

Dr. Stephen Hawking without compromise said that "There was nothing around before the Big Bang" [13]An interesting comment. How this could be proved is very interesting. It has not been proved. It is only, at best, a guess.

Arnold Penzias (Physics Nobel Prize Co-Winner for the discovery of the cosmic wave background) has said that" Astronomy leads us to a unique event, a universe which was **created** out of nothing".

Really? The cosmic wave background tells us that our universe was created out of nothing?

Stephen Hawking has categorically stated "There was **nothing** around before the Big Bang"[13]. Dr. Hawking is omniscient? He and Leonard Mlodinow, in their book *"The Grand Design [14]"* state that their book was written "to give the answers that are suggested by recent discoveries and theoretical advances" and to inform us that "**we have a great many universes created out of nothing".** This is Exactly what Dr. Krauss said: word for word.

Theoretical physicists and "thinkers" could not even agree what "nothing" meant when they met March 20, 2013 at the American Museum of Natural History. The simple idea of "nothing", a concept that even toddlers can understand, proved surprisingly difficult for them (Neil DeGrasse Tyson, Lawrence Krauss, Jim Holt, Charles Seife, Eva Silverstein and Max Vilenkin) to pin down, with some of them questioning whether such a thing as nothing exists at all[23]

Dr. Neil DeGrasse Tyson said at this meeting that "Maybe 'nothing' will ever be resolved".

He may be right.

Are the "simple, elegant, laws of physics" responsible for "nothing"?

Michio Kaku, Professor of theoretical physics at New York University says that "No one knows who wrote the laws of physics or knows where they came from. Science is based on testable, reproducible evidence, and so far, we cannot test the universe before the big bang". Since we have absolutely no insight what the laws of physics might have been at time, we can't possibly have any insight as to how they were involved in the formation of our universe".

He may also be right.

Dr. Sean Carroll, California Institute of Technology, has admitted that "cosmologists.... sometimes exaggerate a little bit about what it (the big bang, sic) means" (admitted on a *Science Friday publication*).

He may be right.

In this author's opinion, the proof of a big bang cannot be presented as fact without empirical evidence of its occurrence! **And so far, there is *no* empirical evidence- the big bang is simply a set of uncorrelated observations.**

This author does not believe that "nothing" can become "something" or "everything". What do you believe? Can "nothing" become "something"?

Dr. Neil DeGrasse Tyson agrees when he says that "Nothing is not nothing. Nothing is something. That's how a cosmos can be spawned from the void"[31] He has written a review of Dr. Krauss' book which includes many other opinions from individuals in many other academic disciplines. Many reviewers have classified this discussion as a "kerfuffle" (a lot of argument, noisy activity, or fuss). He continues to say that "It's a shame when smart people who agree about most important things can't disagree about some other things without throwing around insults. We should strive to do be better than that". He further admits on *Science Friday* that "cosmologists.... sometimes exaggerate a little bit about what it (the Big Bang, sic) means.

He may be right.

Dr. Stephen Hawking without compromise said that "There was nothing around before the Big Bang" [13]An interesting comment. How this could be proved is very interesting. It has not been proved. It is only, at best, a guess.

Arnold Penzias (Physics Nobel Prize Co-Winner for the discovery of the cosmic wave background) has said that" Astronomy leads us to a unique event, a universe which was **created** out of nothing".

Really? The cosmic wave background tells us that our universe was created out of nothing.

The idea of a universe from nothing is an interesting idea, but hardly provable using the scientific method. It would require lots of speculation to even suggest that "nothing" was necessary for the formation of our universe. It is a nonsensical idea.

According to Dr. John Lennox, "What all this goes to show is that nonsense remains nonsense, even when talked by world-famous scientists. What serves to obscure the illogicality of such statements is the fact that they are made by scientists; and the general public, not surprisingly, assumes that they are statements of science and takes them on authority" and that "**immense prestige and authority does not compromise faulty logic**[20]".

So where are we now? Nowhere. What evidence do we have that was obtained using the scientific method? **There is no experimental physics that can prove that something can come from nothing. and we cannot prove that there was an explosion.** Odenwald believes that the big bang was **not** an explosion.[26]

So, who do you believe? And why? There is so much more we need to know in order to answer our questions with any degree of accuracy.

Belief is a critical component of truth.

CHAPTER EIGHT

LIFE ON EARTH

HOW DID IT GET HERE?

It would appear that this chapter has nothing to do with the formation of our universe- **but it does.**

Some theoretical physicists and cosmologists believe that life on Earth is made up of "stardust" (see *"The Stardust Revolution"* a book written by Jacob Berkowitz[2]) which was scattered throughout our universe **as a direct result of the big bang**. How one could "prove" this assertion is unknown. How could you know that all matter on Earth is the result of "stardust" created by the big bang?

Are there other "ideas" about how life arrived on Earth? Yes, there are. The possibilities are briefly explained as follows:

1. Spontaneous Generation

Spontaneous generation (abiogenesis) is the idea that living matter on Earth came from non-living matter. This idea was disproved by Louis Pasteur in 1864 using his famous "Swan Necked flask" experiment in which he proved that "Life is a germ, and a germ is life".

In the 1920's Haldane and Oparin re-opened the idea of spontaneous generation. They stated that "spontaneous generation of life on Earth would take too long to accomplish and therefore would leave little supporting evidence in its favor- therefore it was not possible".

In 1953, Stanley Miller and his graduate student Harold Urey showed that Glycine -the simplest amino acid known could be produced in the laboratory under simulated conditions of primordial Earth- **or at least what they believed to be the conditions of primordial Earth** [s] This experiment has been repeatedly confirmed and today still remains verifiable. But were the laboratory conditions they used the same as those that existed on primordial Earth? How could they possibly have any idea what primordial Earth conditions were like? They could not. They were just guessing.

2. Out of The Ocean and onto the land.

This is the concept that atoms of Carbon, Hydrogen, Nitrogen and phosphorous in the Earth's primordial oceans grouped together to form organic coacervates (an aggregate of colloidal droplets held together by electrostatic attractive forces during an "acelluar" era). These coacervates later grouped together and formed a "membrane" around them initiating a "cellular" era. Presumably the molecules inside these membrane bound coacervates grouped together to form more complex molecular arrangements found in living matter, which eventually formed a life form that allowed them to move out of the water and on to the land where more complex plant and animals were formed (the concept of evolution of life on Earth). There is nothing mysterious about this concept. **You either believe it or you do not believe it. If you do believe it, you must ask what evidence is there for this, and was this evidence obtained using the scientific method?**

2. Panspermia (literally means "Seeds Everywhere")

Panspermia is the belief that life on Earth was "seeded" from space [Wikipedia]. The Swedish chemist Arrhenius theorized that bacterial spores were propelled through space by light pressure, landing on Earth, which ultimately developed into living matter. A Theory? No, this is just a guess.

Panspermia remains unanswered and is not a concept taught in academia today. A hypothesis has not even been proposed that can be tested to support this guess. There is no credible experimental evidence to support this idea.

As a matter of fact, if life came to Earth in this manner, where did the life originate from that eventually reached Earth?

3. Directed Panspermia

Directed Panspermia is the belief that life originated elsewhere in our universe and that some form of intelligence was responsible for its journey to the planet Earth.

This is also a guess.

Crick and Orgel, staunch supporters of Directed Panspermia, did **suggest** that an intelligent civilization could have arisen elsewhere in our universe, and that this intelligent civilization could have built a spaceship and seeded our universe with life[5] Suggest anything you wish to suggest. Suggestions require only imagination.

4. "The *"Stardust Revolution: The New Story of our Origin in The Stars"*

This is the idea that we are all made up of stardust. It was first introduced by Carl Sagan in one episode of his 1980's "Cosmos" series.

A book written by Jacob Berkowitz titled *"The Stardust Revolution"* [2] suggests that all living (and non-living) matter on Earth is made up of "stardust". There is no credible experimentation to support this idea. This is also a guess.

This book states that "stardust is the merging of the once-disparate realms of astronomy and evolutionary biology, and of the Copernican and Darwinian Revolutions, placing life in a cosmic context".

The Stardust Revolution takes readers on a grand journey that begins on the summit of California's Mount Wilson, where astronomers realized that the universe is both expanding and evolving, to a radio telescope used to identify how organic molecules, the building blocks of life, are made by stars".

Perhaps. This author cannot find any credible evidence that the building blocks of life are "made by stars". The building blocks of life are generally considered to be amino acids and nothing more that is more complex than sugars, proteins, and nucleic acids.

Berkowitz continues to say that "Today an entirely new breed of scientists-astrobiologists and astrochemists-are taking the study of life into the space age", believing that stardust is "the missing link towards the formation of all that we see around us and was the precursor to the cosmos' first solids-the first step towards the formation of rocky planets".

This book is more than 300 pages in length, in which you will be confronted with what the stardust "revolutionists" want you to **believe**. Whether you believe what *they* believe is up to you. *It's all about belief. There is no scientific evidence to support this idea.*

Marcus Chown wrote the following in his 2000 book *The Magic Furnace* [4]

"Many of the most dramatic and awe-inspiring of cosmic events-from the violent death throes of stars to the titanic fireball that gave birth to the entire universe 15 billion years ago- *are connected to us directly by way of the atoms that make up our bodies"*, and that "we first needed to realize that atoms were actually made and **not** put in the universe on Day One by *the Creator"*.

"The **creator**" is indicative that a creator **was** present, but He had no role in the formation of our universe.

Chown's assertions are at best speculations and assumptions. But there are others that believe this. The only way that Chown's assertions are provable is to trace an elements movement from where it came from and its subsequent appearance on earth, either in living or nonliving matter. This, of course has never been done, and probably cannot be done ("Tracing" of radioactively labeled molecules is routinely done in biochemistry research, but it requires

identification of that same radioactive labeled element in different molecules as they move from one molecule to another. This is not an easy task to do). The movement of a labeled atom from our sun and then identifying it in an "earth" molecule (living or nonliving) is an impossible task.

David J. Eicher in his book "*The new Cosmos-Answering Astronomy's Big Questions*" tells us that "*We know that life exists on Earth. And life exists here because our star, the sun, made it so*" [10]We do not know this as truth. There is no scientific proof of Eicher's belief.

Do these **beliefs** make the formation of life on our planet out of "stardust" a fact? No, they do not,

5. Creation

No one has an absolute answer to the question was our universe created by God or were the laws of physics and the use of mathematics responsible for the formation of our universe.

Remember what Dr. John Lennox said in his book titled "**Gods Undertaker- Has Science Buried God?** [19] that" **there is no more important debate than <u>science</u> versus <u>religion</u>. But it needs to be reborn again, with a clear understanding of what science and religion really are, which is not an easy task to do".** He continues to ask questions in his book "God and Stephen Hawking- Whose Design Is It Anyway?" [20]

Science is defined as "**The intellectual and practical activity encompassing the systematic study of the structure and behavior of the physical and natural world <u>through observation and experiment</u>**" Wikipedia

Religion is defined as "**A unified system of beliefs and practices relative to sacred things** Wikipedia

Remember that Albert Einstein said "**Science without religion is lame; Religion without science is blind**" [3] This statement is supportive of Einstein's belief that science and religion must work together in order to understand how both contribute to each other.

Paul Davies in his book *God and The New Physics* [6] attempts to explain how God and the "new" physics are intertwined, and further attempts to explain God and science in his book *The Mind of God-Science and The Search for Ultimate Meaning* [8]

Dr. Neil DeGrasse Tyson in his book "*Astrophysics for People in a Hurry*" [30] has aptly asked the following: "At one time or another every one of us has looked up at the night sky and wondered: What does it all mean? How does it all work? And, what is my place in the universe"? These questions are very broad in scope, and certainly do not have universally accepted answers. He further states that "In this slim volume you will earn a fundamental fluency in **all the major ideas** and discoveries that drive our understanding of the universe".

In this "slim volume" we will earn a fundamental understanding of our universe? What a relief this is!

Dr. Tyson goes on to ask "What happened before all of this? What happened **before** the beginning?

Astrophysicists have no idea and that **astrophysicists have little or no grounding in experimental science** ". This seems to be a defeating statement - on one hand detailed information is presented as to how our universe was formed, right down to the first nanoseconds of time, and then on the next hand we are told that astrophysicists have no idea what actually happened because they have little or no grounding in experimental science? He goes to state that "some religious people assert, with a tinge of righteousness that something must have started it all: a force greater than all others, a source from which everything issues. A prime mover. In the mind of such a person, that something is, of course, God." A list provided by Dr. Tyson in this book provides us with nine "cosmic perspectives" One of these cosmic perspectives is that "the cosmos is spiritual, even redemptive- but not religious".

What do you **believe**? Is there a "prime mover"? There is no doubt that our universe is here, and that it must have had a beginning. But to boldly state that **"everyone of our bodies atoms is traceable to the big bang and to the thermonuclear forces within the high-mass stars that exploded more than five billion years ago"** and that **"we are stardust brought to life"** is an astounding statement.

This is nothing more than a personal belief and has no basis in science at all.

The "academic elite" are, however, identified by Dr. Tyson as "slightly more clever than other humans" and are "capable of doing theoretical astrophysics and other rudimentary calculations in their head, like their little Timmy who just came home from preschool".

Hawking and Mlodinow [14] have made their positions clear about creation by saying "**The universe is not created by God**", that "**Physics leaves no room for God**", they have "**Shown God to be unnecessary**", "that '**science is the only way to truth**", and that "**Mathematics is the ultimate solution to all of our questions**". Dr. John Lennox offers a challenge by saying that "only the gullible profess to be able to answer" and believes that "**we have a duty to point out that not all statements made by scientists are statements of science, and so do not carry the authentic science even though such authority is often erroneously ascribed to them**"

Dr. Lennox's challenge is a bold and necessary challenge!

Most theoretical physicists do not believe that God created our universe. Most do not even use the word creation to describe the formation of our universe. Instead they use the word "origin" (which is an incorrect word use).

Origin is defined as "the point or place at which something comes into existence or the point or place where something comes from" Wikipedia. The "point" or "place where our universe came from has not been identified. The theoretical physicist will, however, deny this by telling us that our universe did not originate from a point- its origin was "everywhere".

So, what is "the bottom line"?

Here it is: ***Until theoretical physicists can prove beyond a shadow of a doubt that matter was present at the site of the big bang one must conclude, without reservation, that our universe must have been formed in some other unexplained way- and this they cannot do. They only say that we have identified the early composition of our universe- and then back track" to what they think might have been.***

There is only one other possibility for the formation of our universe: **Creation** by the hand of God as described in the Holy Bible.

Are there any references in the Holy Bible about the formation of our universe by a "big bang" or a "singularity"? No, there is not. But does this mean that a creator was, or was not involved in the formation of or universe? No, it does not.

Would it be necessary for the Holy Bible to include details about an event such as a big bang? Not necessarily.

Would it be necessary for a God that is omnipotent, omnipresent, and omniscient to let us know everything in great detail about the formation of His universe? Not likely, as this would remove Him from the realm of omniscience.

So, what is "creation"? The Hebrew word for creation is "Bara" and the Hebrew word for "making something" is "Asah". There is evidence in the Holy Bible for God doing both of these- creating **AND** making. Hank Hannegraff has answers to most of the pertinent questions about creation in his book *The Creation Answer Book*.[11]

Remember, that "origin" and "creation" have different meanings in the English language:

Origin is defined as:

The point or place at which something comes into existence or the point or place **where** something comes from. It has nothing to do with "creation",

Creation is defined as:

1. "The act of ***making*** or producing something ***that did not exist before***" or

2. "The act of ***making*** something that has ***never been made before***"

While the Bible does not give us a detailed description how our universe was formed, it does provide us with numerous references about its ***creation***.

Genesis 1:1-3 says that "In the beginning God created the heavens and the Earth. Now the earth was formless and empty, darkness was over the surface of the deep, and the spirit of God was hovering over the waters. And God said, "Let there be light", and there was light.

So, there was **no** light *until* God ***created i***t.

Hebrews 11:3 says that "By faith we understand the universe was formed at God's command, so that what is seen was ***no***t made out of what was visible."

So, the universe was formed at God's command and that He ***created*** the universe from materials that were ***not*** visible.

Proverbs 3:19-20 says that "By wisdom the Lord laid the Earth's foundation, by understanding He **set the heavens in place**; by His knowledge the deeps were divided, and the clouds let drop the dew".

So, the heavens (**never before seen)** were put in place by God.

Psalms 19:1 says that "The heavens declare the glory of God; **the skies proclaim the work of His hands.**

No doubt about this. **No mortal can claim how, or why, our heavens are displayed precisely the way they are.**

Psalm 33:6 says that "By the word of the Lord **were the heavens made**, their starry host by the breath of His mouth"

The Lord made the heavens. There is nothing mysterious in the interpretation of this statement.

Job 9:8 says "Who alone **stretches out the heavens** and tramples down the waves of the sea?

Stretches out the heavens is a direct implication that **our universe is expanding.**

Isaiah 40:22 says "It is He who sits above the circle of the Earth, and its inhabitants are like grasshoppers, who **stretches out the heavens** like a curtain and spreads them out like a tent to dwell in".

Stretches out the heavens **is, again, a direct implication that our universe is expanding.**

Isaiah 40:26 says" "Lift up your eyes and look to the heavens: Who **created** all these? He who brings out the starry host one by one and calls for each one of them name by name".

Isaiah 45:12 says "It is I who made the earth and **created** man upon it. *I stretched out the heavens* with my hands, and I ordained all their host".

Stretched out the heavens **is, again, a direct statement that our universe is expanding. The direct creation of man is also stated.**

Isaiah 48:13 says that "Surely my hand founded the earth, and my right hand ***spread out the heavens***. When I call to them, they stand together".

Spread out the heavens is again direct implication that our universe is expanding.

Nehemiah 9:6 says "By His wisdom the Lord has laid the Earth's foundation, by understanding He set the heavens in place; by His knowledge the deeps were divided, and the clouds let loose the dew".

The formation of the Earth the heavens were put in place.

Stretching or spreading out the heavens is mentioned again and again in **Isaiah 51:13, Jeremiah 10:12, Jeremiah 51:15, Psalms 19:1-4, and Zechariah 12:1**

John 1:1-3 says that "Through Him <u>all</u> things were made; without Him nothing was made that has been made".

In other words, God made ALL things. They <u>were</u> *true* creations.

The New International Version of the Holy Bible (**Chapter one, *"Beginning of Early Mankind"***) has this to say about creation:

"Has the universe existed forever? Was there ever a time when it had a beginning?

Surely it must have had a beginning. But when would that have been? How would it all have happened? What made it happen? For what purpose, if any, did it happen?

Who am I? Where did I come from? Why am I here, and how did it all begin?

Since recorded history began, men and women of every generation, culture, and place have searched for answers to these questions. Some say it all happened by *chance*, without any reason or purpose whatever which is somewhat illogical. Chance? What appears to be an intelligent design and order throughout the universe, a formation by chance is hard to accept. And life without meaning seems contrary to the very mind which searches for meaning. So, what are the answers to where did I come from, why am I here, and how did it all begin?"

An objective discussion with most, but not all, theoretical physicists about these questions is impossible. Dr. Lawrence Krauss openly makes fun of religion and the formation of our universe by God (**See the 2009 YouTube video presentation titled *"A Universe from Nothing"***). Dr. Krauss makes it quite clear that he is not interested in religion and, in this author's opinion he is quite sarcastic.

He has a closed mind when it comes to the biblical description of our universe and is not interested in any compromises unless they support **his** beliefs. He really "believes" that "something" can arise from" nothing" (*ex nihilo*) and states that "Modern science is addressing the question of why there is something rather than nothing- with surprising and fascinating results". His opinions about religion and the role of God in the formation of our universe are, in this author's opinion, dogmatic, unprofessional, and unethical.

Of course, Dr. Krauss has the right to believe what he wishes to believe but he, as well las all other theoretical physicists, should make it clear at the outset that their "beliefs" are only **opinions**, and that there is absolutely no reputable scientific evidence obtained using the scientific method to support the belief that "nothing" ever existed, or that "nothing" can become "something".

Read his books and judge for yourself. Look for use of the word "hypothesis"- you will not find it anywhere.

Stephen Hawking and Leonard Mlodinow in their book *The Grand Design* believe that they have "new answers to the ultimate question of life" and state that these "questions are traditionally questions for philosophy, but philosophy is dead".

Really?

Philosophy is dead? Have Hawking and Mlodinow now qualified themselves as experts in the field of philosophy? The question of something from nothing seems to be a pervasive idea about the formation of life on the planet Earth as well as it is about the formation of our universe itself. They continue by saying that a "scientific law is not a scientific law if it holds only when some supernatural being decides not to intervene". Is this a tongue in cheek admission that there is a supernatural being and one that can make decisions?

As an undergraduate student in college, this author took a course in the philosophy of religions. The question "are science and religion compatible?" was a hot topic. My professor was a well-known minister of the Gospel and he allowed heated (but controlled) discussions. One mid-term examination had the following questions we had to answer (they were **not** multiple-choice questions). Try and answer them yourself.

Should we **believe** everything that science asks us to believe? Why?

Are all the "answers" given to us by science **true**? Why?

What is meant by the word "**proof**"?

Do you **believe** in God, which is based upon faith and belief in the Holy Bible?

Do you believe that God and science are **compatible**? Why?

What if you are wrong about God?

This was a tough examination (some of you may remember having answered examination questions in "blue books"). Students answers were later shared (anonymously) in an open classroom discussion. There was never complete agreement but, I believe, this professor opened some minds to a relevant topic.

Most theoretical physicists try to destroy the belief that God created our universe by asking the question: "If there is a God, then who made God?". Answering a question with a question is a typical ridiculous response that provides no answers and leads only to an illogical dead end.

Theoretical physicists also refuse to admit that the Bible is actually a true record of history.

Wait just a minute!! Since the Bible <u>is</u> a true record of history it would be very <u>unscientific</u> to ignore it! *After all, it is the bestselling book in all recorded history.* Theoretical physicists are always complaining about the lack of "evidence" for a creation by God and go to great extremes to "explain" that creation is not an option- and it doesn't matter how weak or strong the evidence may be.

So, is religion and the Holy Bible just nonsense? Not very likely. The fact that the Bible was written by a number of different authors, and the fact that it is very old does not invalidate its contents. Why should its contents be challenged? Students today are taught the principles of Chemistry, Physics, Mathematics, and Astronomy. They accept these principles as truth, and without question. (if they wish to get a "passing" grade). This author does not deny that the "laws" of Physics and the use of mathematics are not useful in certain circumstances. They are in fact useful as long as they are used to examine credible observations - **with an open mind**. This author doubts that any student would pass a course in theoretical physics if they brought up the role of God in the formation of our universe. Nor would they ever use the word creation or introduce the concept of belief in their studies if they wish to be awarded an advanced degree.

Viktor Toth responded to the following question on Quora about creation: "**Are there any other legitimate theories to the creation of the universe, other than intelligent design and the big bang?**"

1. He says that "**Everything' we know about our universe is based upon the 'laws' of theoretical physics and mathematics, and that there is no room for roadside preachers in an explanation for the formation of our universe**".

Roadside preachers? No room for them?

There is a need for "preachers" in the world we live in. They offer interpretations of what is said in scriptures. Theoretical physicists are not equipped to do this any more than a preacher is equipped to offer interpretations of theoretical physics.

2. "**Intelligent design is not a theory. It is a fairy tale created by people who make a living off religion, sold to people who are scientifically illiterate or semi-illiterate**.

Intelligent design (a design by God) is a fairy tale? Fairytales are made up by people using only their imagination. Star Wars", "Little Red Riding Hood", and "The Three Little Pigs" are excellent examples of fairytales.

3 "**The big bang is not a theory about the creation of our universe**"

Of course not. It is only a postulate.

4. "**We don't even know for sure that the universe began at the famous t=0**"

This is true (see "definitions" for t=0 and singularity).

5. "**Without a fully developed quantum theory of gravity, we are groping in the dark**".

Keep on groping. Einstein worked on this until his death with no success. Theoretical physicists are still working on a quantum field of gravity and a unified field theory- with no success.

6. "**Even if we managed to get past these theoretical obstacles, the theory still won't be a theory of the *creation* of the universe. It would be the theory of the evolution of the universe from its earliest moment to the present day and beyond**"

Creation and evolution are quite different. Evolution deals with speciation.

7. "**How, or especially why, the universe came into existence may be a question that should forever remain in the realm of priests and philosophers. But peddlers of intelligent design? We may never know what the theory is, but that does not mean that we can't test it; nonsense apart from real science**".

8. "**There will still be people who refuse to believe (in the "laws" of physics, sic) and cling to their silly religious beliefs**".

Dr. Weinberg says that '**The world needs to wake up to the nightmare of religion.... anything we can do to weaken the hold of religion should be done and may in fact be our greatest contribution to civilization**". He finalizes by saying "**I am utterly fed up with the respect we have been brainwashed into bestowing upon religion" (Stated at the Salk Institute for Biological Sciences in LaJolla, California, 2006).** These words are the words of a Nobel Laureate! They sound like the words of someone who has utter discontent about something they obviously do not believe, do not understand, and do not want others to believe in what they believe.

Dr. Richard Dawkins, writes in his book *The God Delusion*[9] that "**a supernatural creator almost certainly does not exist**" and that "**belief in a personal god qualifies as a delusion**"- which he defines a delusion as "a persistent false belief held in the face of strong contradictory evidence". Really? He also believes that "**when one person suffers from a delusion it is called insanity, and when many people suffer from a delusion it is called religion**".

This author vehemently disagrees. This author believes in God and resents the implication that I, or anyone else that believes in God, is delusionary. Where is the strong contradictory "evidence" that I, or anyone else that believes in God, is delusionary! It is my hope that the contents of his book are read with an open mind, and that readers will make only relevant and positive conclusions about the "theories" of theoretical physicists that are supposedly based upon what Dr. Dawkins calls "evidence".

Many papers written by theoretical physicists, in this authors opinion are desperate attempts to avoid the necessity of a creator.

The Pew Research Center found that "Scientists are roughly half as likely as the general public to believe in God or a higher power", chemists were more likely to believe in God (41%), and that younger scientists (ages 18-34) are more likely to believe in God or a higher power than those who are older *Scientists and Belief Poll, June 2009*

Albert Einstein said the following about God: "I want to know how God created this world. I am not interested in this or that phenomenon, or in the spectrum of this or that element. I want to know his thoughts- the rest are details". He also said in his famous epithet on the "uncertainty principle" that" God does not play dice".

It should be pointed out that many scientists in the past believed in biblical scripture [Wikipedia] Among them are:

Leonardo DaVinci, who is considered by many to be the founder of modern science.

Robert Boyle, the "father" of modern chemistry.

Isaac Newton. the developer of modern calculus.

Louis Pasteur, who demolished the concept of spontaneous Generation

Johannes Kepler, Astronomy

Francis Bacon, the Scientific Method.

Carolus Linnaeus, Biological Taxonomy.

Gregor Mendel, Genetics.

Joseph Lister, Antisepsis.

And the list goes on. It is a list of individuals who were deeply committed to biblical scripture *and* empirical science. In this authors opinion, Krauss, Weinberg, Dawkins, Tyson, Filipenko, Hawking (and probably many other theoretical physicists) have a long way to go before their names may be added to this list.

Predictions, postulates, guesses, ideas, and theories are intriguing, but be careful about **belief**. **Look for the truth!**

God described our universe long before theoretical physicists started trying to convince us that everything in our universe was formed because of the "laws" of physics:

Job 38:31-33 says:

Can you bind the beautiful Pleiades?

Can you lose the cords of Orion?

Can you bring forth the constellations in their seasons?

Or lead out the Bear with its cubs?

Do you know the **laws** of the heavens?

Can you set up God's dominion over the Earth?

SO WHAT DO YOU BELIEVE?

**WHAT YOU BELIEVE OR DO NOT BELIEVE
MAY COST YOU ETERNITY**

EPILOGUE

The purpose of this book was to inform readers about how science goes about the discovery process, why the scientific method is the most critical aspect of the discovery process, and to explain why **belief** is a critical aspect of understanding. When it comes to believing how our universe was formed and that there are only two possibilities to consider about how our universe was formed.

1. By a "Big Bang, and that everything in our universe can be explained by the "laws" of physics and the use of mathematics, or

2. A creation by God. The holy Bible tells us that our universe and everything in it was created by God.

Which do you believe? And why?

This author respectfully suggest that you get a piece of paper and write down your response to the following. Your responses may give you some insight about **your** beliefs regarding the formation of our universe and what your place is in our universe today. Essay answers do not require an essay answer. Simply respond with either a "**Yes**" or "**No**".

Your answers will hopefully establish the foundation for your beliefs about what you are being told today about the formation of our universe and what you may be told in the future.

Do you understand:

1. The meaning of the word "belief"?

2. The difference between "creation" and "origin"?

3. The difference between: A scientific Hypothesis, a Theory, and a Law?

4. The "Scientific Method" (and why it **must** be objectively used to get valid answers to questions?)

Dou you believe:

1. Everything you are told, see and hear from theoretical physicists about the formation of our universe? If not, why not.

2. That the "theories" used by theoretical physicists to explain the formation of our universe are based upon **valid** experimental evidence? Or are they simply guesses or assumptions?

3. That the Scientific Method **is important** in order for scientists to present their "theories" as fact?

4. That there had to be matter for a "big bang" to occur?

5. That the universe we live in was **"nothing"** when a Big Bang supposedly occurred – but then ultimately nothing became "something" and then "everything" in our universe as we know it today?

6. That everything in our universe-both living and non-living is made up of stardust?

7. That Panspermia or Directed Panspermia are responsible explanations how life got on Earth?

8. That a great deal more evidential and credible evidence must be obtained using the scientific method in order to prove that matter was present at the site of the big bang in order to have a better understanding of the formation of our universe?

9. That our universe was created by God?

10. That our universe was created only because of "the laws of physics" and mathematics can answer all of our questions about the formation of our universe??

11. That faith is an important aspect of belief?

12. That "Belief" is an important part of our everyday life?

13. That truth is a necessary component of belief?

14. That truth is a necessary component of scientific research?

These "belief" questions could go on and on. You can probably come up with a few more on your own.

What do you believe?

We all have the right to believe what we want to believe about how our universe was formed. This author is not a physicist tor a mathematician, so I am not in any position o challenge in this respect.

It appears that most theoretical physicists "believe" that the laws of physics and mathematics have all the answers to our questions about the formation of our universe and that *God had no part in its formation.* While this author is in no position to challenge them about the "laws" of Physics, Mathematics Astronomy or Cosmology, I can, however, challenge them about their beliefs, assumptions, maybes, perhaps, and the proper use of linguistics and semantics.

This author is also not fearful of rejection or criticism. **Theoretical physicists and cosmologists can no more prove that matter was present and necessary for a "Big Bang" to occur than can I prove that our universe was created by God.**

We do **not** have all the answers. Theoretical physicists and cosmologists will, however, continue to come up with new "theories" (some justifiable and some not justifiable). They will continue to gather valid evidence about certain aspects of Astronomy, Physics, Chemistry, and Biology- but the argument about a big bang-and whether or not matter as we know it was necessary for the formation of our universe will continue.

As I have openly stated, this author believes that God created our universe, and that He has let us discover what we presently know and that He will let us "discover" more only as He deems necessary and appropriate.

No one will ever convince this author that "nothing" or "something" or simply "energy" was the only thing necessary for the creation of our universe, that we are all here because of Panspermia, or that everything on Earth is made up of stardust.

No one will convince me that because I believe in God that I am delusionary.

Are there compatible areas for science and religion? In my opinion there are, but there is a lot more work that needs to be done in order to solidify compatibility. Scientists who are pursuing answers to this question and the question about whether or not there is life somewhere else in our universe have a lot more work that needs to be done.

We should all <u>listen</u> to words and <u>not just hear them</u>, and try to understand what they mean, and use them correctly in the English language. If this is not done, our present day understanding (or misunderstanding) of the formation of our universe, and all life on earth, could lead all of us into a "black hole".

So how did out universe begin? There is no absolute answer to this question.

How will our universe end? There is no absolute answer to this question.

Will the human species on Earth be the cause of our own demise? There is no answer to this question.

Will our universe end with the collision of our Milky Way galaxy with the Andromeda galaxy? There is no answer to this question.

When will God decide to return Jesus to our planet? There is no answer to this question. Only God knows.

The purpose of this book was to provide you with the information you need in order to understand, and challenge, what you think about what you are being told by theoretical physicists about the formation of our universe.

Regardless of who you are, or what you believe, you should seek only the truth.

REFERENCES AND IMPORTANT BOOKS

1. Alcock, James E (2018), *Belief: What It Means to Believe and Why Our Conviction Are So Compelling*, Prometheus Books

2. Berkowitz, Jacob (2012), *The Stardust Revolution-The New Story of Our Origin In The Stars*, Prometheus Books.

3. Calaprice, Alice (1996). *The Quotable Einstein*, Princeton University Press.

4. Chown Marcus (2001), *The Magic Furnace*, Oxford University Press.

5. Crick, F.H.C. and L.E. Orgel (1973), *Directed Panspermia*, Icarus 19:341-346

6. Davies, Paul (1983)4 *God & The New Physics*, Simon and Schuster.

7. Davies, Paul (1992), The Mind of God, Penguin Books

8. Davies, Paul (1993), *The Mind of God-Science and The Search For Ultimate Meaning*, Penguin Books.

9. Dawkins, Richard (2006), *The God Dilusion*, Bantom Press.

10. Eicher, David J. (2015), *The New Cosmos- Answering Astronomy's Big Questions*, Cambridge University Press

11. Hanegraff, Hank (2012), *The Creation Answer Book*, Thomas nelson Publishing.

12. Hubble, Edwin P. (1929), A Relation between Distance and Radial Velocity Among Extra-galactic Nebulae, Proc. Nat. Acad. Sci., 15:168-173

13. Hawking, Stephen (2009), *The Theory of Everything*, Jaico Publishing House.

14. Hawking, Stephen and Mlodinow, Leonard (2010), *The Grand Design*, Bantam Books.

15. Hawking, Stephen (1996), *A Brief History of Time*, Bantam Books

16. Jogalekar, Ashutosh (2014) .*Falsification and its Discontents*, The Curious Wavefunction.

17. Kennedy, D.J. (1999*), Why I Believe*, Thomas Nelson Publishing, Inc.

18. Krauss, Lawrence M.(2012), *A Universe From Nothing*, Simon and Schuster.

19. Lennox, John C. (2009), *God's Undertaker-Has Science Buried God?*, Trafalgar Square Publishing

20. Lennox, John C. (2011), *God and Stephen Hawking- Whose Design It Anyway?*, Lion Books

21. Lerner, E., Bucking The Big Bang, New Scientist 182 (2448) 20, 22 May 2004

22. Lisle, Jason (2011), *Taking Back Astronomy*, Master Books.

23. Moskowitz, Clara (2017), *What is Nothing? Physicists Debate*, Live Sciences.com

24. Novella, Steven (2018), *The Skeptic's Guide To The Universe*, Grand Central Publishing

25. Popper, Karl (1963), *Science as Falsification*, Excerpts, Conjectures and Refutations.

26. Odenwald, Sten, *Why The Big Bang Is Not A Explosion*, Washington Post, May 14, 1997.

27. Russel, Bertrand (1993), *The Quotable Betrand Russell*, Amherst, NY:Prometheus

28. Sarfarti, Jonathan (2014), *Refuting Compromise*, Creation Book Publishers

29. Thornhill, Wall (2004, An Open Letter To The Scientific Community, New Scientist, May 22, 2004

30. Tyson, Neil deGrasse (2017), *Astrophysics For People In A Hurry*, W.W. Norton and Company

31. Tyson, Neil deGrasse and Goldsmith, Donald (2004), *Origins-Fourteen Billion Years of Cosmic Evolution*, W.W.Norton & Company.

32. Weinberg, Steven (1993), *The First Three Minutes*, Basic Books, A Member of the Perseus Books Group

33. Wieland, Carl (2006), *Creation*, Secular Scientists Blast The Big Bang

Books Group.

If I have overlooked someone I apologize.

Printed in the United States
by Baker & Taylor Publisher Services